MOSAICS
In An
Afternoon

MOSAICS
In An
Afternoon

By Connie Sheerin

Sterling Publishing Co., Inc.
New York

PROLIFIC IMPRESSIONS PUBLICATION STAFF

Editor: Mickey Baskett
Copy: Phyllis Mueller
Graphics: Dianne Miller, PrePress Xpress
Photography: Greg Wright
Administration: Jim Baskett
Styling: Laney Crisp McClure

ACKNOWLEDGEMENTS

Many thanks to the following companies for their contributions of supplies for this book:

For Make-It-Mosaics Products, FolkArt® Acrylic Paints, and Decoupage Finish:
Plaid Enterprises, Inc.
P.O. Box 7600
Norcross, GA 30091-7600
Website: www.plaidonline.com

For wooden pieces:
Walnut Hollow
1409 State Road 23
Dodgeville, WI 53533
800-950-5101

For small colored glass pieces (Cobbles):
Optimum Glass Company
P.O. Box 1632
Greeley, CO 80632
800-619-7355
E-mail: mosaics99@aol.com

For grout and grout sealer:
Custom Building Products
Polyblend Grout
13001 Seal Beach Blvd.
Seal Beach, CA 90740
1-800-272-8786

For adhesives:
Signature/Beacon Adhesives
301 Waganaw Rd.
Hawthorne, NJ 07506
973-427-3700
E-mail: crafts@intereach.net

For tiles:
Orlandini Tile Company
Walnut & Pine Streets
Marcus Hook, PA 19061
610-494-7107

For small tiles, unusually shaped tiles, glass, recycled flatbacked marbles:
Crafts a la Cart
85 W. Baltimore Avenue
Lansdowne, PA 19050
610-394-0992
E-mail: Concraft@aol.com

Every effort has been made to insure that the information presented is accurate. Since we have no control over physical conditions, individual skills, or chosen tools and products, the publisher disclaims any liability for injuries, losses, untoward results, or any other damages which may result from the use of the information in this book. Thoroughly read the instructions for all products used to complete the projects in this book, paying particular attention to all cautions and warnings shown for that product to ensure their proper and safe use.

Published by Sterling Publishing Company, Inc.
387 Park Avenue South, New York, N.Y. 10016
Produced by Prolific Impressions, Inc.
160 South Candler St., Decatur, GA 30030
© 1999 by Prolific Impressions, Inc.
Distributed in Canada by Sterling Publishing
c/o Canadian Manda Group, One Atlantic Avenue, Suite 105
Toronto, Ontario, Canada M6K 3E7
Distributed in Great Britain and Europe by Cassell PLC
Wellington House, 125 Strand, London WC2R 0BB, England
Distributed in Australia by Capricorn Link (Australia) Pty. Ltd.
P.O. Box 6651, Baulkham Hills, Business Centre, NSW 2153 Australia
Printed in China
All rights reserved
Sterling ISBN 0-8069-5775-1

Library of Congress Cataloging-in-Publication Data

Sheerin, Connie.
    Mosaics in an afternoon / by Connie Sheerin.
        p.   cm.
    Includes index.
    ISBN 0-8069-5775-1
    1. Mosaics--Technique.   I. Titles.
TT910.S44 1999
738.5'6--dc21   98-50986
                                                    CIP

Dedicated to the memory of my loving and very creative sister, Gwen.

A Special Thanks...

To my husband, Ken Williams, the "good husband," who spent many a lonely night, never complaining, while I worked in the studio until the wee hours, and who has refined his skills in ordering out for yummie dinners...for both of us!

To my mother, Ginnie Fischer, and my father, Ted Fischer, who bought me every available arts and crafts product to play with while growing up.

To my daughter, Alicia Sheerin, who has put up with her very unconventional mom all these years with hardly a complaint—well, maybe one or two!

To my dear friends for many years, Ann Rogers and Terri Ruckert, without whom I could not have ever finished this book.

To my former student and new friend, Carla D'Iorio, whose love for mosaics brought her help on many late nights.

To my oldest and dearest friend, Joanne Marincola, who always believes in me, encourages me, and knows I can do even more!

A Word of Encouragement From Connie

I hope this book will convince you that making mosaics is fun, easy, and rewarding. Please understand that I use the word "mosaics" in the very broadest sense. In no way are my mosaics an attempt to recreate the incredible works of art from the past. For me, mosaics are like putting together a puzzle, using bits and pieces of mixed media and color to create interesting, attractive designs. I have fun making them, and I believe anyone can be successful with my kind of mosaic designs.

Take a look at the different projects in this book. They are made with readily available materials, and they don't take a lot of time to do. Start with something small and, before you know it, you will see flat surfaces in every nook and cranny of your home as possible surfaces for creating mosaics.

I have tried to present a variety of projects—ones that will interest an artist who has already done mosaics and ones for beginners looking for a start. I hope you will find one that's just right for you.

Reach back to the child artist within you, and remember—have fun! ∞

About the Artist

Connie Sheerin has crafted in one way or another for as long as she can remember. Although she majored in communications, she earned spending money in college doing pastel portraits of her friends.

While looking for her first real job, she took a night school class in crafts. The instructor, who owned a small craft shop, was looking for a manager, and hired Connie. Connie stayed in the crafts industry—designing, demonstrating, and teaching—until her daughter, Alicia, was born. Wanting to be a stay-at-home mom, Connie staged in-home craft parties, ran holiday craft sales at her home, and sold her design work to different manufacturers.

After she divorced, Connie wanted to be with her daughter as much as possible, so she began a program called Crafts a la Cart, an in-patient crafts program in 10 area hospitals. She and several friends then opened a retail store, Crafts a la Cart Studio, offering an array of crafts supplies and classes.

During that time, Connie began doing live TV in the Philadelphia area as the Crafts Lady, bringing viewers a new craft each week. Eventually, she was producing, directing, and starring in five-minute craft segments called "Connie's Craft Quickies," which she marketed to over 50 television stations. Recently she has been a guest demonstrator on numerous television programs, including *The Rosie O'Donnell Show*, *The Carol Duvall Show*, *Home Matters*, *Handmade by Design*, and *Willard Scott's Farm & Garden Journal*.

After spending 10 years working in public relations and marketing special events, Connie tired of the fast pace and traveling and returned to the craft industry in 1995. Today, she designs, writes, and has resurrected Crafts a la Cart, which is now a multi-level at-home workshop business she formed with two partners. It gives creative women a chance to teach while developing their marketing and business skills, as well as, the chance to obtain financial freedom.

Her favorite craft is mosaics, and her project book, *Creative Mosaics*, was published by Plaid Enterprises in 1998. She is a member of the Society of Craft Designers and is very happy to reach a broader audience with *Mosaics in an Afternoon*.

Connie resides in Lansdowne, Pennsylvania with her husband Ken Williams, a therapist who works with adolescents, and her studio sidekick, Angel, a teacup yorkie. "Life is good," Connie says. "I am blessed to be able to work at what I really love—turning my dreams into creative realities." ∞

CONTENTS

WHAT ARE MOSAICS?

Mosaics are designs or pictures made by piecing together material such as tile or glass. This art form has been created since ancient times by people all over the world.

A Brief History

The first mosaics, created thousands of years ago by the Sumerians in Mesopotamia, were made of terra cotta cones. Pebbles were used to create mosaic pavements in the gardens of ancient China and on floors of houses in Turkey and northern Greece. The Greeks cut natural stone into small triangles, squares, and rectangles called *tesserae*. (Today, the word tesserae is used to describe all types of materials used to make mosaics.) The style was embraced by the Romans, who by 200 A.D. were beginning to create mosaics on walls as well as floors. Cut glass pieces were commonly used to create the early Christian mosaics.

In the Byzantine era, from the fifth to the 15th centuries, mosaics were created to cover entire walls and ceilings, and in the 15th and 16th centuries, important Italian painters designed mosaics for the great cathedrals, including St. Peter's Basilica in Rome. By the 18th century, Rome was a center for mosaic art. Vatican artists began producing miniature mosaics—jewelry, small pictures, and boxes—using *smalti filati*, threads of opaque glass cut into tiny shapes. The Art Nouveau movement of the late 19th century revived interest in mosaics on the exteriors of buildings with an emphasis on pattern and design, especially in the cities of Barcelona, Prague, and Paris.

How I Got Started

My interest in mosaics started with wonderful Pennsylvania Dutch quilts made by my mother and grandmother. I distinctly remember examining all the patterns and colors in the quilt on my bed over and over again; I can still see some of the swatches when I close my eyes. I believe this is where I found my interest and fascination with putting together colors and shapes and sizes to form a beautiful piece of art.

My beginning "mosaics" were made with beans and seeds I found in my mother's kitchen. Later I used different kinds of pasta, coloring them with paint and making designs with the different colors and shapes. At the Summer Arts & Crafts Program at our local playground I made wonderful coasters and trivets and covered tin cans (which became pencil holders) with fabulous little tiles that came glued to a webbed sheet. Many kids glued the sheet down just as it came and grouted it, and they were finished. Not me! I picked off the different colors from the webbed backing, drew a design, and filled in the design with tiles, one at a time, and then grouted. I won ribbons for the best mosaics of all the playgrounds at the end of the summer! I was hooked.

Because tiles weren't readily available and I found quilting too precise and tedious, I began doing collages using all sorts of materials. And the fascination continued. However, it wasn't until years later, when I found a source for all colors and shapes of tiles, that I made my first round coffee table top—6' in diameter—for my home. It was a monumental project, and I just loved doing it. I made smaller items until the tiles ran out, and then life got in the way.

Twenty years later I began collecting tiles and broken china and bits and pieces of colored glass and flatbacked marbles and decided it was time to begin again. This time, I used all the materials I had gathered to create mixed media mosaics, adding three-dimensional molded pieces I made from craft plaster as the focal points of my designs. Shells and beach glass are other wonderful additions.

Keep in mind that mosaic materials such as glass, tiles, and china—even seashells—will last a long time, and your mosaic could become a family heirloom. Be certain to sign and date all of your pieces—they're likely to be around 100 years from now! ∞

WHAT ARE
MIXED MEDIA MOSAICS?

Mixed media mosaics are those that include not only flat materials such as tile and glass but also shards of china and pottery, stones, shells, chunks of glass, flatbacked marbles, buttons, and cast plaster pieces. Mixed media mosaics can be flat and level on the surface, like traditional mosaics, or three dimensional or a combination of the two, with three dimensional pieces surrounding a flat area or with a flat area surrounding three dimensional pieces.

Decorative mosaics created with broken materials—tile, glass, and china—are called "picassiette" after Maison Picassiette, a cottage in Chartres, France that was built in 1929 by Raymond Isidore (1900-1964), a foundry worker, cemetery caretaker, and road repairman. Isidore spent 35 years covering the surfaces of his cottage—outside and inside, including all of the furniture and a woodstove—with shards of colorful crockery, glass, stones, and shells. His neighbors gave Isidore and his house the name "picassiette." The approximate English translation is "stealer of plates," but is also supposedly a play on the words "Picasso of plates." A variation of the term, "pique assiette," could be loosely translated "crazy plates."

Although many picassiette mosaics are created from randomly arranged, randomly broken pieces, others are made by carefully and systematically breaking a piece of china and then reconstructing it in a specific way that preserves the look of the china pattern and creates a unique picassiette design. ∾

Mosaic Materials

Finished mosaics can look complicated, but mosaic techniques are simple to learn and many mosaic projects are quick and easy to do. Many mosaic materials are readily available and inexpensive, and some materials—such as broken china, seashells, and beach glass—are free or cost very little.

ALL YOU NEED ARE:

- **Tesserae** are tiles, glass pieces, broken china or terra cotta that are pieced together on a surface to create the design
- **Surface**, such as wood, terra cotta, plaster, or metal
- **An adhesive**, such as white craft glue or a silicone adhesive, to hold the tesserae to the surface
- **Grout**, to fill the spaces between the tesserae, smooth the surface, and add strength and durability to the mosaic
- **Tools**—a few simple tools such as tile or glass nippers and a rubber mallet. ∾

How to Estimate How Much
Material You'll Need

There are several ways to estimate how much mosaic material you'll need to complete a particular project. Experience is the best teacher, and it is, of course, better to have too much than not enough. Here are some guidelines and tips.

Some artists and crafters just buy lots of tiles—more than they think they'll need—knowing they'll use what's left eventually. When you're beginning, it's good to have some extra tiles on hand, especially if your design calls for precise cutting or nipping.

Another option is to measure the project and multiply the dimensions of the mosaic area to determine the size of the mosaic in square inches or, for really large mosaics, in square feet. If you're working only with tiles, a close estimate is possible because when tiles are sold by the package or the sheet, the coverage in square feet or square inches is noted for the consumer.

If you're creating a mixed media mosaic, you can do a rough estimate based on the dimensions of the finished piece minus the amount of coverage provided by the china or terra cotta or plaster pieces. It's also possible to estimate how much material you'll need for a mixed media design by roughly laying out the design on the surface or—if you're using a pattern—on the pattern, allowing space between the pieces for grout. This is easy to do on a flat surface, but all surfaces aren't flat. If the surface isn't flat, measure the dimensions (if it's a bowl, for example, measure the height and the circumference), draw a diagram of the surface area using those measurements on graph paper or brown kraft paper, and lay out the material on the paper diagram.

For most of the projects in this book, the mosaic area size is given in square inches. Some projects are fairly precise in what's required; for others, the final design is up to you. If a design uses whole tiles of a specific size, the size and number are noted. If broken tiles are to be used, the size of the tiles can vary, and the number needed would too.

When working in mixed media, the number of broken plates or broken tiles needed to cover a space varies, depending on many factors, including the size of the plate, how big the design area is, and how usable the broken pieces are. If you're creating a mosaic on a table or a lamp, the table or lamp you want to use may not be the same size as the one I used. Feel free to improvise. ∞

Closeup of "Deco Dreams Table" — *instructions on page 78.*

Ceramic Tiles

Ceramic tiles are made from clay or china that has been shaped in a mold and fired. They are available in a huge array of shapes, sizes, and colors, individually and on sheets, decorated and plain, glazed and unglazed. The color of the tile may be due to the color of the clay it is made from or from a glaze that is applied before firing. Some tiles have painted designs; you can also paint or stencil your own designs on tiles with permanent enamel paints. Tiles may have a textured or smooth surface and a glossy or matte finish.

Tiles can be bought at crafts and building supply stores and specialty stores that sell tile and bathroom fixtures. ∞

Glass & Mirror

You also can create mosaics using only pieces of glass (some early mosaics were made only of small, opaque glass cubes) or with a combination of tiles, broken china, glass, and mirror.

- *Glass Tiles*

    Glass tiles are small squares of stained or clear glass. They are typically sold in packages in crafts stores and stores that sell mosaics supplies.

- *Stained Glass*

    Stained glass pieces, cut in shapes with a glass cutter or broken into irregular pieces, can be used to create mosaics. Stained glass pieces are available from crafts stores and catalogs. Because stained glass is generally not as thick as tiles, you may wish to build up the surface under the glass pieces with silicone adhesive so they will be flush on the surface with thicker tiles if you use glass and tile in the same mosaic piece. The unpolished edges of glass pieces are sharp and dangerous if not grouted.

continued from page 14

● *Polished Glass*

Polished glass pieces are pieces of irregular clear glass and colored textured glass that have smooth, polished edges, so they're safe to handle and use. They are typically sold in packages in crafts stores. These are great to use for ungrouted mosaics and they are also effective with grouting.

● *Beach Glass*

Beach glass or "beaten glass" are pieces of glass you can find on the beach. They are likely pieces of broken bottles that have been pounded on the beach by the surf, resulting in a frosted appearance and smooth edges. You can also find commercially produced beach glass.

● *Mirror*

Mirror pieces can be found as small square "tiles" or in larger sizes that can be broken into irregular shapes. Various thicknesses are available. You can buy mirror glass at crafts and department stores and from dealers who specialize in glass and mirror.

● *Marbles*

Flatbacked marbles are available in a wide range of clear and opalescent colors. They are made by melting and cooling glass pieces—when the molten glass cools on a flat surface, it assumes a rounded shape on the top while the bottom conforms to the flat surface underneath. Flatbacked marbles are available at crafts stores and from stores and catalogs that sell supplies for stained glass. ∞

CAUTIONS

Use care when cutting, breaking, and handling glass. Edges are sharp. Wear gloves, goggles, shoes, and protective clothing. Be sure to sweep your work area carefully to get up any stray shards, splinters, or chips. Don't let children handle glass with unpolished edges. ∞

Mixed Media

Mixed media mosaics can be made of broken china, seashells, molded plaster pieces, or terra cotta. I have found many of the pieces I have used in my home, my friends' homes, secondhand shops, yard and tag sales— even the trash! Soon you'll have a wonderful collection. Ask your friends and neighbors to save broken china and flower pots for your mosaics. You can reward them with a mixed media mosaic piece as a gift!

• China

Broken china pieces can come from plates, bowls, cups, or saucers. Plates or saucers are the best sources because they will break into flat pieces. Store the pieces in a jar until you're ready to use them.

• Pottery

Terra cotta pieces come from broken clay flower pots and saucers. **Broken pottery** can also create interesting looks for your designs.

• Shells

Seashells can be found at the beach for free or purchased at crafts stores. Mosaics are the solution for what to do with those leftover souvenirs of beachcombing.

• Buttons

Buttons can also be used. Everyone has a jar of old buttons—mosaics are a great place to use them.

• Plaster

You can make **molded plaster pieces** or buy them. To make them, you'll need plaster or candy molds and craft plaster—all available at crafts stores. Follow the package instructions for molding and drying. ∾

CAUTIONS

Use care when cutting, breaking, and handling broken china. Edges can be sharp. Wear gloves, goggles, shoes, and protective clothing. Be sure to sweep your work area carefully to get up any stray shards, splinters, or chips. Don't let children handle broken china pieces with unpolished edges. ∾

Back Boards & Surfaces

• Ceramics & Plaster

Terra cotta pots and planters are excellent surfaces for mosaics. An additional benefit is that the mosaic further insulates the pot, protecting the plant's soil from drying out. You can purchase **plaster** surfaces such as frames and trivets at crafts and ceramics stores or mold them yourself with craft plaster. **Cement** stepping stones, decorated with mosaics, add a personal touch to your garden or patio. You buy them at garden supply stores or mold them yourself. Buy the molds at crafts stores. **Glazed** ceramics or china can also be used as a base for your designs.

• Metal

Metal trays, pitchers, and bowls also are good surfaces for mosaics. Clean before using and sand to remove rust and rough spots. Look for great deals at tag and yard sales and thrift stores.

• Glass & Mirror & Plastic

You can create mosaics on trays made of glass or mirror or sturdy plexiglass. Look for sturdy pieces with smooth edges at yard sales and thrift stores. You can also have pieces of glass or mirror or hard plastic cut to shape at glass and mirror dealers. Choose material that is 1/4" thick and have them polish the edges smooth. Use stick-on felt pads on the bottom.

• Wood

Wood surfaces such as unfinished furniture and accessories such as frames, wall shelves, and plates can be purchased at crafts, department, and furniture stores. Furniture pieces such as tables and chairs and accessories—bookends, candlesticks, bowls, and boxes, for example—can be found at yard and tag sales, auctions, and thrift stores. Flat mosaic pieces also can be built on plywood or fiberboard that has been cut to any shape. You can buy plywood and fiberboard at building supply stores.

Wood surfaces that will receive mosaics should be sealed with a clear acrylic sealer and allowed to dry before tesserae is applied.

• Papier Mache

Sturdy papier mache items, available at crafts stores, are also suitable surfaces for mosaics. Seal the surface before applying the tesserae.

Adhesives & Grout

• Adhesives

A variety of adhesives can be used to glue tesserae to surfaces. The one you choose depends on the base and the mosaic materials you are using—the adhesive should be compatible with both surfaces. The two adhesives used extensively in this book are white craft glue and silicone adhesive.

White craft glue can be used for gluing flat materials (tile, flat glass, flatbacked marbles) to flat, horizontal surfaces. It holds the pieces securely, dries clear and flattens as it dries, leaving room for grout between the tile pieces

Silicone adhesive works best on curved surfaces or vertical surfaces. Because it is thick, it will hold pieces in place while drying. However, it does not flatten, so you must be careful that you don't use too much or that too much does not "ooze" between the tile pieces, leaving no room for grout. It's also the adhesive of choice when gluing for ungrouted mosaic effects. Silicone adhesive also is useful when you're using materials of different thicknesses and you wish to build up the thinner material to be level with the others.

A craft stick is a convenient spreader for glues and adhesives. *Don't* use your finger!

Mastic is a ready-to-spread adhesive sold by the bucket or the container that is applied with a trowel. Mastic is suitable for mosaics that will be used outdoors. It is generally used on large, flat surfaces (like walls) but can be used on smaller pieces like backsplashes and stepping stones. Follow manufacturer's instructions for application. Mastic is available where tile is sold.

Always read the manufacturer's instructions on glue and adhesives packages and follow all precautions and warnings. Many glues give off fumes as they dry. Avoid inhaling them and work in a well-ventilated area or outdoors.

• Grout

Grout is the material that fills the spaces between the tile, china, and glass pieces, adding to the strength and durability of a mosaic piece. Grouts are made of Portland cement; some grouts also contain polymers, which contribute additional strength and flexibility.

Tile grout is available two ways: non-sanded and sanded. **Non-sanded grout** is preferred for mosaics with crevices up to 1/4" wide, especially those made of material that is easily scratched. **Sanded grout** is just that—grout with sand added to

it. Use it for mosaics with larger crevices (more than 1/4"). Grout is available by the container and by the pound at crafts, hardware, tile, and building supply stores.

Grout can be purchased in more than 30 colors, ready to mix with water. If you want a strong color, buy colored grout. Adding a colorant to white grout and getting a really strong color is nearly impossible.

White grout can be colored with **liquid or powder colorants**—you mix the colorant with the grout while you're preparing it. Mix powdered colorant with the grout powder before adding water; mix liquid colorant with the water before adding the water to the grout. Options for coloring grout include concentrated food dyes, acrylic paints, herbs, glitter, and spices.

You also can color the grout after it has dried on your mosaic with liquid fabric dyes (natural and otherwise) or strong coffee or tea. Experiment with the dye on pieces of dried grout to check the color before you apply it to your finished piece.

Mix grout in a **small plastic bucket** or a **disposable plastic container**, following the instructions on the grout package. (It should be the consistency of nut butter or fudge.) If you want to use your mixing container again, clean out the leftover grout before it dries and rinse the container thoroughly. Using a disposable container is handy—you can throw it (and your leftover grout that's in it) away when you're finished. I like to use plastic yogurt containers. Wear gloves to apply grout.

Don't pour leftover grout down the sink or flush it down the toilet—it can clog your pipes. If you are sensitive to dust, wear a mask when mixing grout.

Use a **sponge** to wipe away excess grout from the surface of the mosaic. Keep a bowl of water nearby to rinse and squeeze out the sponge often as you wipe. Wear gloves to protect your hands.

When the grout has dried, you can smooth the edges with **sandpaper**. Sandpaper can also be used to remove grout from a surface where it doesn't belong.

• Sealers

Grout sealer is a clear liquid that comes in a bottle or can. Apply it with a brush to seal the grout to protect it from stains and the elements. Sealing is recommended for table tops (to protect them from stains) and for mosaics—especially flat surfaces—that will be used outdoors. Buy it where grout is sold. ∞

Tools

Only a few simple, inexpensive tools are needed for creating mosaics. Many of these you may already have around your home.

• *Nippers*

For cutting or breaking tiles, glass, and china, you'll need **tile nippers** or **glass nippers**. They look and are handled much like pliers—some have sharp blades and others have round disks and they have spring action handles. To use them, grasp the material you want to cut or break with the nippers. When the blades or disks are pressed together, they will crack and break the material. Choose nippers that feel comfortable in your hand. *Caution: Always use goggles when nipping pieces of tile, ceramic, or glass.*

• *Mallet*

I use a **rubber mallet** to break plates or large numbers of tiles into irregular pieces. Some people use a *hammer*, but I don't—with a mallet, you have more control and the pieces won't break into such tiny shards and dust.

• *Spreaders*

Use **craft sticks** or **plastic spreaders** to spread adhesives on the surface or to apply adhesives to individual tiles. They can also be used to fill grout into tight places or used to smooth grout on edges.

To spread grout over the glued tesserae, use a **rubber spatula** or a **plastic putty knife**.

• *Tweezers*

A pair of long-handled **tweezers** can be of help when you're placing small pieces.

• *Brushes*

A **foam brush**, **bristle paint brush**, or **artist's paint brush** can be used to paint trim and backgrounds for mosaic designs. When the grout has begun to dry, use a **stiff bristle brush** to brush away the excess.

• *Miscellaneous*

For mixing grout, you'll need a **measuring cup** to measure the water.

Use a **damp sponge** to wipe away excess grout. Have a **bowl** (stainless steel or plastic) of water nearby to rinse the sponge as you wipe.

Use a **ruler** for measuring when you want to make a precise cut. ༄

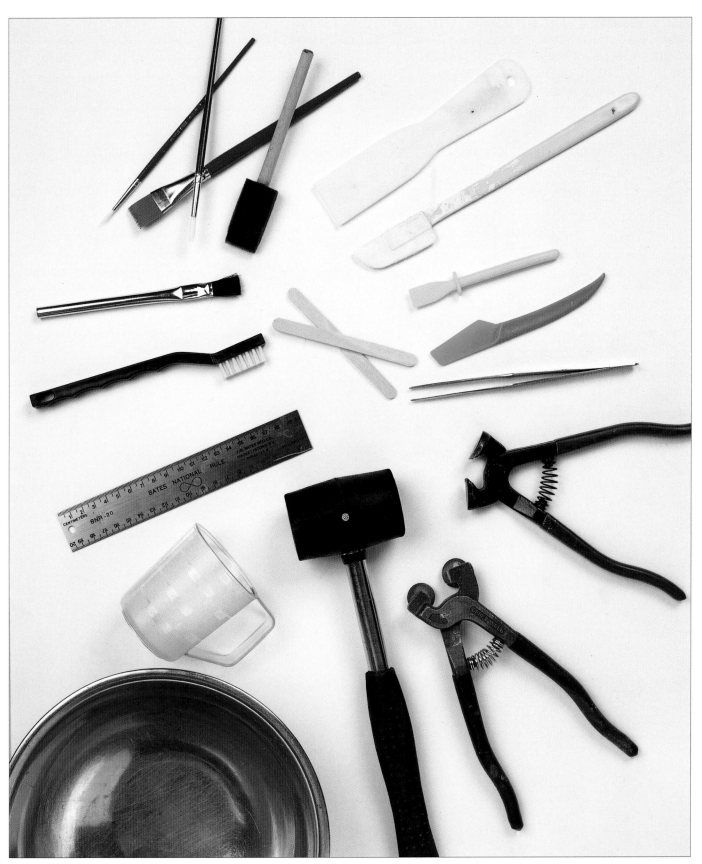

Protective Gear

Mosaic materials break into sharp pieces and have sharp edges. Until you become used to handling them, be especially cautious.

Protect your eyes when cutting and breaking tiles and china by wearing **protective goggles**. Wear **latex gloves** when grouting so you won't cut your fingers on any sharp edges and so the grout won't dry out your hands.

They're shown in this photo with a **tile cutter**, which is used to score and break precise, straight cuts on flat tiles, especially ones thicker than 1/4". ∞

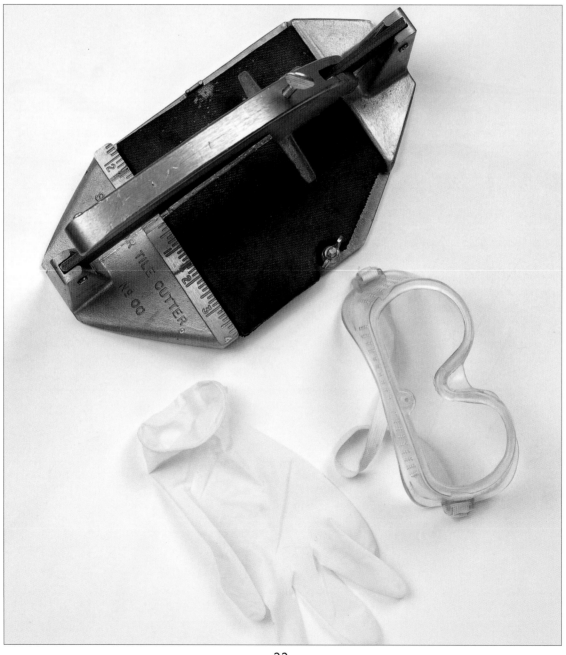

Pattern Drawing & Other Supplies

• *Pattern Drawing Supplies*

To draw your own designs, you'll want **graph paper** or brown kraft paper for making patterns, a **ruler**, a **circle template** for drawing round shapes and curves, and a **pencil**. You'll find them at crafts, arts supply, and office supply stores.

Use **transfer paper** to transfer your designs to surfaces. After transferring, go over the outline of the design with a **permanent black marker** so the lines will be easier to see once you have spread the glue and are filling in with the tiles.

• *Other Supplies for Creating Mosaics*

Other supplies used for the projects in this book can be found at crafts stores.

Permanent enamel paints can be used to decorate plain tiles. The colors are painted or stenciled on, then baked in the oven.

Acrylic craft paints are used to paint trim areas and surfaces.

Stencils can be used with permanent enamel paints to create designs on plain tiles.

Metallic rub-on wax can be used to enhance molded plaster motifs, grout, and painted wood. Apply it with your always-available tool—your finger. (I find nothing works quite as well.) You can remove what's left on your finger when you're finished with nail polish remover. ∽

THE DIRECT
MOSAIC TECHNIQUE
FOR PATTERNED TILE DESIGNS

The direct technique is the easy—what you see is what you get. The tile is cut to size and glued face up on the surface. When the glue dries, the piece is grouted. This colorful frame that I am using as an example of the technique is a fun project that's easy for beginners. You'll need enough tile to cover about 40 square inches.

PROJECT SUPPLIES

Wooden frame, 7" x 9"
Square tiles, 3/8" and 7/8", in 10 different colors
4 round tiles, 1", in various colors
7 round tiles, 1/2", in various colors
3 round tiles, 5/8", in various colors
White craft glue
Clear acrylic sealer
Non-sanded grout - white

TOOLS & OTHER SUPPLIES

Sandpaper, 220 grit
Circle template; Ruler; Pencil
Black permanent marker; Graph paper
Tile nippers; Safety goggles
Glue spreader or craft stick
Plastic container; Latex gloves
Rubber spatula; Measuring cup
Sponge; Stiff bristle brush; Soft cloth
Metal or plastic bowl

Project pattern on page 31

Prepare Surface & Transfer Design

1. All surfaces should be oil-free and clean. To prepare a wooden surface, sand lightly to be sure the area where the tiles will be glued is even and to smooth any part of the surface that will be painted. Wipe or brush away sanding dust.

2. Seal the areas of the wood where you're planning to glue the tile with clear acrylic sealer to protect them from the moisture of the grout. Let dry.

3. Draw the design to size on graph paper (**photo 1**) or, if you're using a pattern, trace the pattern on tracing paper. Using transfer paper and a stylus, transfer the design to the surface.

Photo 1

Prepare Tiles

4. Using tile nippers, nip square tiles into a variety of smaller shapes (**photo 2**). Just nip about 1/8" and the tile will snap across. They will not always break perfectly—don't be concerned! That's part of the beauty and forgiving nature of mosaics. *To break a large number of tiles,* place the tiles between layers of newspaper, in a brown grocery bag, or inside a thick plastic bag. Use a rubber mallet to strike the tiles and break them into smaller pieces. Don't overdo it though, or you'll end up with tiny shards and dust.

Photo 2

Photo 3

Attach Tiles
to the Surface

5. **Spread Glue**: Working one small section at a time, spread glue on the project surface with a rubber spatula or a craft stick (**photo 3**). It's also a good idea to spread glue on the backs of the larger tile pieces for better contact and adhesion.

6. **Place Tiles**: Place the key design pieces (in this case, the circular tiles) first. Then position the remaining tiles, one section at a time (**photo 4**).

7. **Nip to Fit As You Go Along**: As you place the tiles, nip pieces to fit as needed (**photo 5**). This is like putting the pieces of a puzzle together. Remember they don't have to fit perfectly—that's what grout is for!

Photo 4

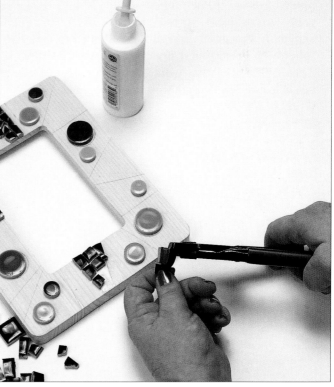

Photo 5

Grout The Design

8. **Mix:** Measure grout and water in a plastic container, following package instructions (**photo 6**). With experience, you'll learn to judge how much grout you need to mix.

  - How much grout you need depends on the size of the piece and close together the pieces are. A larger mosaic, of course, requires more grout than a small one. A mosaic piece where the tiles are farther apart will require more grout than a piece of the same size where the tiles are placed closer together.

  - You can buy colored grout or mix in a colorant. If you're using a colorant, mix it in as you mix the grout.

  - You can't save unused grout if you mix too much, so if you're not using a colorant, mix a little at a time, use that, and mix more as needed. If you're using a colorant, you need to mix all the grout you need at once so all the grout in the piece will be the same color.

Photo 6

9. **Spread Grout:** Using a rubber spatula, a craft stick, or your gloved fingers, spread the grout over the design and push the grout into all areas between the tiles (**photo 7**). Personally, I prefer to use a gloved finger. There is no tool that works better for "feeling" that you've packed the grout into spaces properly.

Photo 7

28

Photo 8

10. **Wipe:** Fill a bowl with water. Dampen a sponge, squeezing out excess water. Wipe away excess grout. Be sure there is grout between all the tiles. If you notice a hole, fill with grout, then wipe.

11. Rinse the sponge, squeeze out excess water, and wipe again. Do this over and over until all the tile pieces are visible through the grout (**photo 8**). Wipe gently but thoroughly. Allow to dry 15 minutes.

12. **Brush:** Before the grout is completely dry, brush away any "crumbs" of grout with a stiff bristle brush—you can use a throwaway bristle brush or old toothbrush (**photo 9**). Let dry completely.

13. **Polish:** As the grout dries, a haze or film will form over the tile. When the piece is completely dry, polish off the haze by rubbing with a soft cloth (**photo 10**). The tiles or glass will return to a beautiful gleam.

Photo 9

Photo 10

Finish the Piece

14. Sand the edges of the frame with sandpaper to smooth the edges of the grout and to remove any stray grout from the sides of the frame (**photo 11**). Wipe away dust.

15. Paint the edges of the frame with acrylic craft paint, using a foam brush (**photo 12**). You may want to use a smaller brush for this. Also, be sure to paint the inside edges where the mirror will reflect the wood.

Note: You can also choose to paint your project surface before beginning mosaics. If you do this, you may need to touch up the paint after mosaic has dried. I do whatever method seems best for a particular project. ∽

Photo 11

Photo 12

Tile Frame Pattern
(Actual Size)

Mixed Media Technique with Random Placement

Tiles, molded plaster pieces, flatbacked marbles, and the broken pieces of a floral patterned china plate are combined to make this mosaic frame. After the plaster pieces and flatbacked marbles are glued in place, the space around and between them is filled with randomly placed broken china, whole tiles, and pieces of tile. The size of the mosaic area is 33 square inches.

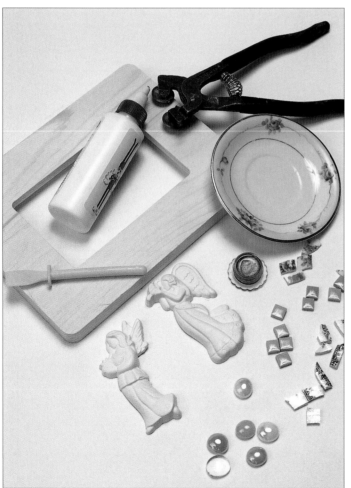

Photo 11

PROJECT SUPPLIES

Wooden frame, 6" x 8"
15 square pink tiles, 3/8"
9 flatbacked opalescent marbles, pink and white
China plate with pink floral motifs and gold border
Plaster molds:

    Right-facing angel   Left-facing angel
    Large star   Medium star

Craft plaster
Gold metallic rub-on wax
White craft glue
Acrylic craft paint - pink
Non-sanded grout - white
Grout colorant - pink

TOOLS & OTHER SUPPLIES

Sandpaper, 220 grit
Newspaper
Rubber mallet
Tile nippers
Safety goggles
Glass nippers
Glue spreader or craft stick
Plastic container
Rubber spatula
Metal or plastic bowl
Sponge
Latex gloves
1" foam brush

Prepare the China

1. Place the china plate between several thicknesses of news-paper (**photo 1**).

2. Hold a rubber mallet at a slight angle above the plate between the thicknesses of newspaper (**photo 2**). Hit the plate with the mallet. The plate will break into large pieces. *Be sure to wear safety goggles.*

3. Lift newspaper occasionally to check the size of the pieces (**photo 3**). Keep smashing away until the pieces are easy to handle and close to the size you want.

Photo 1

Photo 2

Photo 3

4. Break china into smaller pieces or pieces of specific sizes and shapes with glass nippers (**photo 4**). Be careful—the pieces can be sharp—wear gloves and safety goggles.

Prepare Plaster Pieces

5. Mold plaster pieces, following instructions on the plaster package.

6. When dry, molded plaster pieces can be painted with paints made specifically for painting plaster or with acrylic craft paints (**photo 5**).

7. For an easy metallic finish for your plaster pieces, rub on gold metallic wax for gleam and shine (**photo 6**).

Photo 4

Photo 5

Photo 6

Attach Pieces to Surface

8. Glue plaster pieces and flatbacked marbles in place. Spread glue on backs of larger pieces (**photo 7**). For smaller pieces, spread glue on project surface.

9. Fill in the space between and around the plaster pieces and marbles with broken china, whole tiles, and broken tiles. Use photo as a guide. Attach all pieces. Let dry.

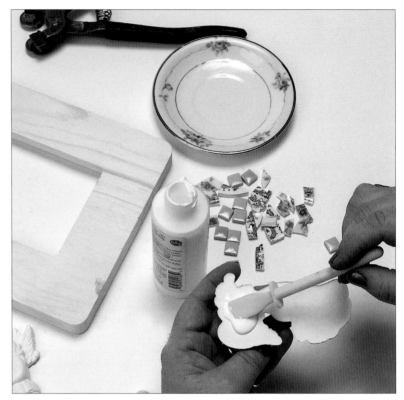

Photo 7

Grout the Design

10. Mix dry grout with water in a plastic container, using proportions specified on the grout package. If you want colored grout, mix dye colorant with grout according to package instructions (**photo 8**).

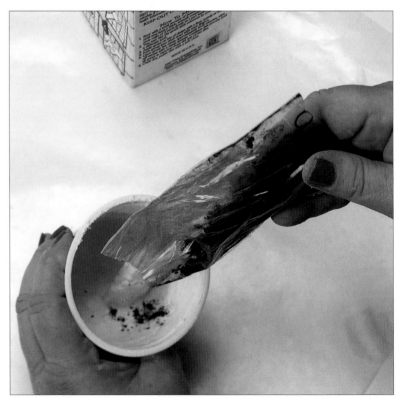

Photo 8

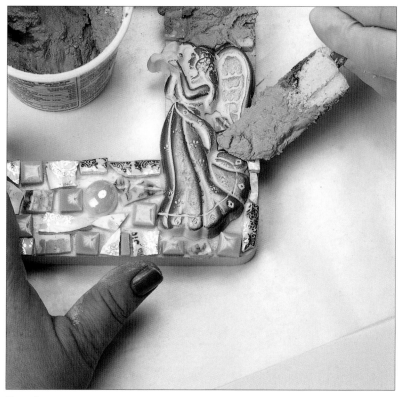

Photo 9

11. Spread grout around the plaster pieces and over the tiles and broken china, using a rubber spatula (**photo 9**). Try to keep grout off the tops of the plaster pieces.

12. Wipe away excess grout with a damp sponge. Let dry about 15 minutes.

13. Brush away grout crumbs with a stiff bristle brush. Allow project to dry completely.

Finish the Project

14. Polish the piece with a soft cloth.

15. If, in applying the grout, some of the paint or metallic wax is removed from a plaster piece or grout gets lodged in a crevice of a plaster piece, touch up the plaster with paint or metallic wax after the grout has dried (**photo 10**).

16. Paint the edges of the frame with pink paint. ∾

Photo 10

MOSAICS
ON CURVED SURFACES

Creating a mosaic on a curved surface is a challenge that's easily accomplished by using a full-bodied adhesive, such as a silicone adhesive, as a glue. The adhesive fills the space between the curved project surface and grabs it, keeping the flat tiles from sliding while you work. Be sure to read and follow the adhesive manufacturer's instructions and cautions and work in a well-ventilated area.

PROJECT SUPPLIES

2 white ceramic pots, 5" and 6" diameter (or terra cotta pots painted white)

1 terra cotta pot, 4" diameter

125 square tiles, 3/8", for the 6" pot:
- Green
- Teal
- Cream

40 square tiles, 1/2", for the 5" pot:
- Red
- Dark Blue
- Light Blue
- Mauve

30 square tiles, 1/2", for the 4" pot:
- Light blue
- Turquoise
- Teal
- Green
- Peach

Clear Silicone adhesive

Gold metallic rub-on wax

Dried leaves and flowers in several colors

Clear acrylic varnish

Non-sanded grout - buttercream

White craft glue

Decoupage finish

TOOLS & OTHER SUPPLIES

1" foam brush

Toothpicks

Glue spreader, such as a craft stick

Rubber spatula

Plastic gloves

Decoupage scissors

Disposable plastic container

Craft stick

Metal or plastic bowl

Sponge

Measuring cup

Soft cloth

Safety goggles

Prepare Surface

1. Be sure pots are clean and dry. To seal terra cotta pots, apply clear varnish inside and out. Let dry.
2. Apply leaves and flowers to sides of pots, using photo as a guide for placement or creating your own designs.
   - Trim the leaves and flowers with decoupage scissors as needed to complete your design.
   - Apply decoupage finish to surface of pot where you wish dried flowers and leaves to be placed.
   - Press the leaves and flowers firmly with a damp paper towel, being sure there are no air bubbles. Use paper towel to wipe away excess finish.
   - If the flowers start to lift, use a toothpick and some white glue to glue them back down.
3. Apply two to three coats clear acrylic varnish to the sides of the pot over the leaves and flowers (**photo 1**). Let dry between coats. Let final coat dry completely.

Prepare Tiles

4. Measure the circumference of the pot and decide how many tiles you'll need to circle the rim by dividing the circumference in inches by the width of the tiles in inches. (Approximate numbers for each pot are listed with Project Supplies.)
5. Select the tiles, choosing pleasing combinations of colors, to be glued in rows around the tops of the pots (**photo 2**).

Attach Tiles

6. Spread the silicone adhesive on one section of the rim of the pot (**photo 3**).
   - A thick glue such as a silicone adhesive holds the pieces in place on the curved surface and dries quickly.
   - Use enough glue to hold the tiles and fill the gap between the flat back of the tile and curved surface of the pot, but don't use so much that the glue fills the spaces between the tiles or squishes up between the tiles.
   - Remove any excess adhesive that squishes up between the tiles with a toothpick while the adhesive is still wet.
7. Place tiles on rim over glue (**photo 4**). Add more glue, then more tiles, working around the rim. Check the spacing of the tiles as you get near the end; you may need to place the tiles just slightly closer together or just slightly farther apart to get a good fit. Let glue dry.

Photo 1

Photo 2

Photo 3

Grout

8. Mix grout in a plastic container, following package instructions.
9. Wearing a protective glove, spread the grout over the design and push the grout into all areas between the tiles (**photo 5**). Try to keep the grout on the rim and not on the sides of the pot. If you get grout on the sides of the pot, wipe away immediately.
10. Wipe away excess grout with a damp sponge. Allow to dry about 15 minutes.
11. Wipe away grout crumbs with a stiff bristles brush.
12. When the grout dries, there will be haze or film over the tile. Polish the haze off with a soft cloth.

Finishing

13. Rub gold metallic wax on the top edge of each pot. ∞

Photo 4

Photo 5

UNGROUTED
MOSAIC EFFECTS

You also can create interesting mosaic effects without grout, using polished glass pieces, which are available in clear, iridescent, and a variety of colors. In the ungrouted mosaic technique, the glass pieces are arranged on a surface and attached with clear adhesive.

PROJECT SUPPLIES

2 wood photo frames, 4" x 5"
Gold spray paint
Clear Silicone adhesive
Clear and iridescent polished glass
    pieces
Purple, blue, and green polished glass
    pieces
Sandpaper, 220 grit
Tweezers

Prepare Surface

1. Sand frames lightly. Wipe away dust.

2. Spray both frames with gold paint, being sure to achieve complete coverage. Let dry completely.

3. Apply silicone adhesive to a section of one frame (**photo 1**).

Place Glass Pieces

4. Arrange glass pieces over silicone adhesive.

5. Apply adhesive to another part of the frame and arrange glass pieces (**photo 2**). Use photo as a guide for placement. Repeat, working around the frame until the surface is covered with glass pieces. (Be sure to remove any excess adhesive before it dries—once dry, it is nearly impossible to remove.)

6. Add a second layer of glass pieces to partially cover the first. You will find tweezers helpful when placing smaller glass pieces. See photo for placement ideas. Let dry.

7. Use the same technique to apply glass pieces to the second frame. In these examples, the frame on the right was decorated with clear and iridescent glass pieces, and the frame on the left was decorated with colored glass pieces. ∞

Photo 1

Photo 2

Glass-Studded Candle Holder

The candle flame flickering through the colors of the glass looks like fireworks! Beautiful!

SUPPLIES

Metal candle holder from a thrift shop
   or yard sale
Polished glass pieces in a variety of
   sizes
Flatbacked marbles in a variety of
   colors
Silicone adhesive
Gold spray paint
(Optional): Sandpaper

INSTRUCTIONS

1. Be sure the candle holder is clean,
   dry, and free of rust. If needed, rub
   with sandpaper to smooth any rough
   spots. Wipe away dust.
2. Spray with gold paint. You may need
   to apply several coats for thorough
   coverage. Let dry completely.
3. Glue a layer of glass pieces on the
   candle holder, working one area at a
   time. Let dry.
4. Glue flatbacked marbles and additional glass pieces on candle holder,
   using photo as a guide for placement.
   Let dry. ∞

Wonderful Projects
for Your Home

Mosaics are at home in almost any decor, and many pieces are suitable for outdoor use. In the pages that follow, you'll find instructions for more than 35 projects you can make for your home, porch, and garden. There are fabulous frames and furniture pieces, an array of items for your table, backsplashes for the bathroom, and bottles for the boudoir. Find them all on the following pages under these categories:

- *FRAMEWORK*
- *WALL & FLOOR*
- *FURNITURE & ACCESSORIES*
- *COLORFUL CONTAINERS*

Each project includes step by step instructions and a list of tesserae and other supplies for that project. For most of the projects in this section, you'll also need the basic tools & supplies as listed below.

BASIC TOOLS & SUPPLIES FOR ALL PROJECTS

Keep the following tools and supplies on hand for each of the mosaic projects you create.

Tile nippers
Rubber mallet
Glue spreader or craft stick
Plastic container for mixing grout
Rubber spatula
Measuring cup

Sponge
Metal or plastic bowl
Stiff bristle brush
Soft cloth
Safety goggles
Latex gloves

Reflected Beauty

This gorgeous mirror will be the showpiece of your decor. It will look great in so many areas—your entry hall, above a mantle, in the bathroom, or over a dressing table. Find a flat wooden frame as your base.

Method: Mixed Media
Mosaic Area: 450 square inches

SUPPLIES

Mirror in wooden frame, 24" x 36" with 16" x 26" opening
China plates in flowered prints
Square tiles, 7/8":
  Pink (about 50)
  Green (about 100)
  White (about 50)
24 flatbacked marbles, various colors
White glue
Sanded grout - white
Acrylic craft paint - metallic gold
1/2" foam brush
Clear acrylic sealer
Sandpaper
Tack cloth
Basic tools & supplies

INSTRUCTIONS

Preparation:
1. Sand frame lightly. Wipe away dust.
2. Seal frame with acrylic sealer. Let dry.
3. Nip pink, green, and white tiles in half to create triangles.
4. Break china plates into irregularly shaped pieces.

Attach Tesserae:
5. Using photo as a guide, glue green tile triangles around inner edge of frame.
6. Using photo as a guide, glue white and pink tile triangles, alternating colors, next to green tiles.
7. Glue broken china pieces and flatbacked marbles on frame, placing the pieces randomly.

Grout:
8. Mix grout. Spread over mosaic. Wipe away excess. Allow to dry.
9. Wipe away the haze with a soft cloth.

Finish:
10. Paint the edges of the frame with gold paint. Let dry. ∞

Veggie Delight Frame

Method: Mixed Media
Mosaic Area: 113 square inches

SUPPLIES

Wooden frame, 12" x 14" with a 6-1/2" x 8-1/2" opening
Square tiles, 1":
   Green
   Red
   Yellow
   White
18 flatbacked marbles, 1/2", in various colors
Plaster molds - vegetable shapes and garden motifs:
   Watering can
   Peas
   Corn
   Eggplant
   Bell pepper
   Tomato
   Carrot
   Watermelon
Craft plaster
Plaster paints or acrylic craft paints:
   Light green
   Dark green
   Orange
   Bright pink
   Yellow
   Gray
   Red
   Purple
Transparent gold metallic paint
Plaster sealer - gloss finish
Sanded grout- white
Strong coffee (less than a cup)
Small sponge
Paint brushes for decorative painting
Basic tools & supplies

INSTRUCTIONS

Prepare Plaster Pieces:
1. Mold the plaster pieces according to package instructions. Let dry.
2. Paint with plaster paints or acrylic craft paints, using photo as a guide. Let dry.
3. Paint plaster pieces with transparent gold metallic paint. The paint will settle in the crevices and add shimmer to the plaster pieces.
4. Coat the plaster pieces with several coats of gloss finish plaster sealer to protect them from the grout. Let dry between coats.

Prepare Tiles:
5. Nip green tiles in half to create oblong pieces.
6. Nip red and yellow tiles into pieces about 1/2" square.
7. Break the white tiles into small rectangles in a variety of sizes.
8. Glue green tiles around inside edge of frame.
9. Glue red and yellow tiles, alternating colors, around the outer edge of the frame.

Attach Pieces:
10. Glue the plaster pieces to the frame, using photo as a guide for placement.
11. Glue the flatbacked marbles to the frame, using photo as a guide for placement.
12. Fill in the space between the borders and around the plaster pieces and marbles with white tiles. Nip the tiles as needed to fit. Let glue dry.

Grout:
13. Mix grout and spread over mosaic. Spread the grout right up to **but not over** the plaster pieces—sanded grout can scratch the paint on the plaster. Wipe away excess grout. Let dry.
14. Buff with a soft cloth to remove haze.
15. Tint the grout with very strong coffee, dabbing it on with a sponge until you achieve a tint you like. Let dry.

Finish:
16. If needed, touch up the paint on the plaster pieces. Add another coat of gloss sealer to seal the new paint. ∞

Frames for Mom & Dad

To safeguard your photo, make a color copy of the original and use it in your frame. If you want to hang the picture, you can buy little sawtooth hangers to fit into the back of the frame while the plaster is wet.

Mom's Frame

Method: Mixed Media
Mosaic Area: 28 square inches

SUPPLIES

Plaster frame mold
Back for frame
Square tiles - mauve
White craft glue
Sanded grout - white
5 heart-shaped tiles: Coral, Yellow, Green
Broken floral patterned china plate
Photo or color photocopy of photo
1" sponge brush; Sandpaper; Pencil

Craft plaster
2 decorated tiles - mauve
4 flatbacked opaque marbles
Acrylic craft paint- teal
Sheet of paper

INSTRUCTIONS

1. Make the plaster frame, using the frame mold and plaster, according to package instructions. Let dry. If the plaster has some rough edges when you remove it from the mold, sand the rough spots smooth with sandpaper.
2. Break the china plate and the square mauve tiles into irregular pieces.
3. Using a pencil, draw an outline of the frame on paper. Arrange the decorated tiles, flatbacked marbles, heart-shaped tiles, and broken tiles and china on the paper outline to determine your design, using the project photograph as a guide for placement. When the result pleases you, spread one area of the frame with white glue and transfer the tiles, one section at a time.
4. Mix the grout and grout the frame. Let dry.
5. Polish with a soft cloth.
6. Paint the inside and outside edges of the frame with teal paint. Let dry.
7. Insert the photo in the frame and install the frame back. ∞

Dad's Frame

To make this frame, collect different colored beer caps—the more colorful the caps the more attractive the frame. Choose tiles in complementary colors for the inner edge of the frame. Pebble tiles, which have an irregular outline and some texture on their surfaces, add another interesting look for the center part of the frame.

Method: Mixed Media
Mosaic Area: 28 square inches

SUPPLIES

16-20 beer bottle caps, different colors
Square tiles, 3/8", assorted colors
White craft glue
Sanded grout - buttercream
Photo or color photocopy of photo

Wooden frame, 7" x 9"
Pebble tiles, assorted colors
Silicone adhesive
Red acrylic craft paint
Basic tools & instructions

INSTRUCTIONS

1. Seal the wooden frame. Let dry.
2. Using photo as a guide, glue square tiles around the inner edge of the frame with white glue.
3. Using photo as a guide for placement, glue beer bottle caps to frame with silicone adhesive. Use enough glue to hold the caps securely, but not so much that the glue comes up around the sides of the bottle caps.
4. Glue pebble tiles and other square tiles between bottle caps. Let dry.
5. Mix grout and apply to frame. Wipe away excess. Let dry.
6. Polish away haze with a soft cloth.
7. Paint the inside and outside edges of the frame with red paint. Let dry.
8. Insert the photo in the frame. ∞

Sea Treasures Mirror

Here's a way to use shells and beach glass to make a fabulous keepsake. When you apply the grout to the frame, think of how the ocean washes sand onto the beach. Partially burying the shells with grout gives a realistic look. The curvy edges of the plywood frame are reminiscent of ocean waves.

Method: Mixed Media

SUPPLIES

Baltic birch plywood, 16" x 21", 1/4" thick
Wooden frame, 11" x 12-1/2" with a 5" x 7" opening
Assorted seashells and beach glass
70 square tiles, 7/8", light blue
30 tiles, various shapes and colors
20 flatbacked marbles, various colors
Broken mirror chips
Silicone adhesive
Wood glue
Sanded grout - tan
Scroll saw with #5 blade
Drill with a drill bit slightly larger than the width of the saw blade
Mirror, 5" x 7"
8 window glazier's points
Picture wire, 24"
2 screw eyes
Tracing paper
Transfer paper & stylus
Sandpaper, 100 and 150 grits
Tack cloth
Gloss acrylic craft paint - deep blue
#12 flat artist's brush or 1/2" foam brush
Basic tools & supplies

INSTRUCTIONS

Prepare Wood:
1. Trace pattern. Enlarge on photocopier. Transfer to plywood.
2. Drill a pilot hole in one corner of the mirror cutout. Insert the blade of the scroll saw in the pilot hole. Using the scroll saw, cut out the opening for the mirror.
3. With the scroll saw, cut out the curved edges of the frame.
4. Glue the plywood cutout to the front of the wood frame with wood glue. Let dry.
5. Sand the plywood surface with 100, then 150 grit sandpaper. Remove dust with a tack cloth.

Attach Tesserae:
6. Nip the square tiles in half. Nip some of the halves into quarters.
7. Glue half and quarter tiles around the inside edge of the frame.
8. Using the photo as a guide, glue the lines of tiles in place from the center to the outside of the frame and along the outer edges.
9. Glue shells, beach glass, mirror chips, flatbacked marbles, and remaining tile pieces on the frame. Apply more glue to larger pieces. Let dry.

Grout:
10. Mix 1 cup grout with water according to package instructions. Spread the grout on the frame with a rubber spatula. With gloved hands, push the grout around the tiles and around and under the shells. Mix more grout as needed and spread on frame.
11. Wipe away excess grout with a sponge. Let dry 15 minutes.
12. Brush away excess grout from the nooks and crannies of the shells with a stiff bristle brush or toothbrush. Let grout dry completely.
13. Using a soft cloth, wipe the surface to remove any haze.

Finish:
14. Paint inside and outside edges of frame with deep blue paint. Let dry.
15. Insert mirror in frame and attach with glazier's points. ∽

See pattern for mirror on page 56.

Sea Treasures Mirror Pattern
Instructions on page 54

1 square = 1 inch

Little Treasures Mini Frames

Small plaster frames are decorated with mosaics—with different results. Choose the colors for the mosaics to complement photos of favorite people and pets.

Petal Frame

Method: Direct

SUPPLIES

Frame mold, 4" x 5"
Craft plaster
50 assorted tiles, various colors,
    in leaf, oval, and irregular shapes
White craft glue
Frame back
Sanded grout - beige
Acrylic craft paint - lavender
1/2" sponge brush
Sandpaper, 220 grit
Basic tools & supplies

INSTRUCTIONS

1. Make frame in mold. Let dry. Unmold. Smooth any rough edges with sandpaper.
2. Glue tiles to frame, using photo as a guide for placement. Let dry.
3. Mix grout. Apply to tiles on frame. Wipe away excess, rounding edge as shown in photo. Let dry.
4. Wipe away haze from tiles with a soft cloth.
5. Paint edges of frame with lavender paint. Let dry.
6. Attach frame back. ∽

Domed Tile Frame

Method: Direct
Mosaic Area: 14 square inches

SUPPLIES

Frame mold, 4" x 5"
Craft plaster
Assorted blue tiles, various shapes
White craft glue
Frame back
Sanded grout - gray blue
Acrylic craft paint - royal blue
1/2" sponge brush
Sandpaper, 220 grit
Basic tools & supplies

INSTRUCTIONS

1. Make frame in mold. Let dry. Unmold. Smooth any rough edges with sandpaper.
2. Glue tiles to frame, using photo as a guide for placement. Let dry.
3. Mix grout. Apply to tiles on frame. Wipe away excess. Let dry.
4. Wipe away haze from tiles with a soft cloth.
5. Paint edges of frame with royal blue paint. Let dry.
6. Attach frame back. ∽

Forest Dreams Backsplash

Method: Mixed Media
Mosaic Area: 240 square inches

SUPPLIES

Plywood rectangle, 1/2" thick, cut to fit the space behind your sink (This one is 20" x 12", with the top cut irregularly to follow leaf shapes.)
Leaf shaped tiles, various colors and sizes (approximately 1 lb.)
Blue patterned china plates
Square tiles, 3/8", various colors (to trim top edge—about 120)
Square tiles, 1-1/4":
   Pale gray (about 12)
   Beige (about 12)
Square tiles, 7/8":
   Dark blue (10)
   Yellow (10)
Plaster or candy molds - choose 4 or 5 leaves of different sizes and shapes—you'll make 15 leaves
Craft plaster
Plaster sealer - gloss finish
Acrylic craft paint:
   Light blue
   Gold
   Dark blue
   Yellow
   Brown
Sanded grout - buttercream
Gold metallic rub-on wax
Mastic glue
Glue trowel
Scroll saw
Decorative painting brushes
Pencil
Measuring tape
Basic tools & supplies

INSTRUCTIONS

Preparation:
1. To cut the plywood top shape, position the leaf tiles along the top edge of the plywood rectangle, using photo as a guide. With a pencil, draw around them to create an irregular shape. Remove tiles. Cut shape of top with the scroll saw. Smooth any rough spots with sandpaper.
2. Seal the plywood piece. Let dry.
3. Pour the plaster in the molds to make the leaves. Let dry. Unmold. Smooth any rough edges with sandpaper. Make about 15 leaves in all of different sizes and shapes.
4. Paint the plaster leaves with different colors of acrylic craft paint. Let dry.
5. Rub painted leaves with gold metallic wax.
6. Seal the plaster leaves with three coats gloss sealer. Let dry between coats.

Attach Tesserae:
7. Glue the 3/8" tiles along top edge. Nip tiles as needed to fit.
8. Cut the pale gray and beige square tiles in half diagonally to make triangle-shaped pieces. Glue along the bottom and sides, using photo as a guide for placement.
9. Glue 1" square tiles between the triangular tiles on the sides and bottom.
10. Glue the leaf tiles in place.
11. Arrange the plaster leaves on the plywood base and glue, using photo as a guide.
12. Break the china plates and the remaining square tiles into irregular pieces.
13. Glue china and tile pieces to fill in the areas between the leaves.

Grout:
14. Mix the grout and apply it, trying not to get grout on top of the painted plaster pieces. Wipe away excess. Let dry.
15. Polish the haze away with a soft cloth.

Finish:
16. If the painted plaster leaves are scratched by the grout, touch them up with paint, let dry, rub with metallic wax, and apply another coat of sealer.
17. Paint edges of backsplash with acrylic paint.

To Hang: There are two options. Either use a waterproof adhesive to attach the backsplash to the wall or drill holes in the grout area of the backsplash, screw the backsplash to the wall, and cover the holes with grout. After the backsplash is mounted, caulk the area between the sink or countertop and the backsplash to keep water from seeping in between. ❧

Aquarium Insight
Bathroom Backsplash

The fish can be done in any color to match your decor. The design at the top echoes the shapes of the fish and is reminiscent of ocean waves. Study the project photo to note the various shapes—some of them whole tiles—that have been used to create the bodies of the fish.

Method: Direct
Mosaic Area: 240 square inches

SUPPLIES

Plywood rectangle, 1/2" thick, cut to fit the space behind your sink (This one is 20" x 12".)

Square tiles, 7/8" and 3/8":

Blue	Orange
Black	Green
Red	Yellow

White (You'll need about 70 3/8" tiles for the top border, plus additional white tiles for the design.)

Various tiles in assorted colors—round, triangular, oval, odd shapes

Transfer paper & stylus

Tracing paper

Brown kraft paper

Black permanent marker

Pencil

White craft glue

Non-sanded grout - blue

Permanent ceramic paint:
    Black
    White

Acrylic craft paint - blue

Scroll saw

Sandpaper

1/2" sponge brush

Round artist's paint brush

Clear acrylic sealer

Basic tools & supplies

INSTRUCTIONS

Preparation:

1. Trace the outline of the plywood rectangle on a piece of brown kraft paper. Sketch the placement of the fish shapes inside the outline, incorporating the fish patterns and tile shapes. Use the project photo as a guide.
2. With a pencil, draw an irregular shape along the top edge around the shapes of the fish. Cut out the shape with a scroll saw. Sand edges smooth.
3. Seal plywood surface with clear acrylic sealer. Let dry.
4. Transfer your design to the plywood rectangle. Go over the lines with a black marker.
5. Paint eyes on round tiles that will be the eyes of the larger fish and on some of the elongated oval and odd-shaped tiles that will be the bodies of the smaller fish with permanent ceramic paints. Bake tiles in oven to set paint according to package instructions.
6. Break some of the square tiles into pieces of various shapes.

Attach Tesserae:

7. Glue a row of 3/8" white tiles across top edge.
8. Fill in fish shapes with tiles of different colors and shapes, using photo as a guide.
9. Fill in areas around fish with blue tiles.

Grout:

10. Mix grout according to package instructions and apply. Wipe away excess. Let dry.
11. Polish the haze away with a soft cloth.

Finish:

12. Paint edges of backsplash with blue acrylic paint. ∾

See page 62 - 63 for fish patterns.

Aquarium Insight Bathroom Backsplash
Instructions on page 60

Full size patterns

Vegetable Garden Shelf

This mosaic shelf would be a wonderful addition to a kitchen. Choose tile colors to coordinate with your walls, countertops, and appliances.

Method: Mixed Media

Mosaic Area: To determine the area of your mosaic, first measure the width and depth of the top of the shelf and multiply the two to get the square inches. Then measure the width and height of the apron and multiply. Add the two numbers together. Be sure to have enough tiles to cover that many square inches.

SUPPLIES

Wooden shelf with brackets and apron
Square tiles, 7/8":
  Yellow
  White
  Green
Plaster molds or candy molds:
  Eggplant
  Corn
  Pepper
  Carrot
  Tomato
Craft plaster
Plaster paints:
  Purple
  Green
  Orange
  Red
  Yellow
Acrylic craft paints:
  Yellow
  Green
Transparent gold metallic paint
Plaster sealer - gloss finish
Non-sanded grout - white
Cotton swabs
Sponge brush
Small paint brushes
Sandpaper
Clear acrylic sealer
Basic tools & supplies

INSTRUCTIONS

Preparation:
1. Seal the areas of the shelf where the tiles will be attached. Let dry.
2. Mold the plaster vegetables, following package instructions. Let dry. Unmold. Sand to smooth any rough edges.
3. Paint plaster pieces with plaster paints, using photo as a guide. Let dry.
4. Paint plaster pieces with transparent gold metallic paint. Let dry.
5. Apply two to three coats of gloss sealer to protect the pieces when you grout.

Attach Tesserae:
6. Glue a checkerboard design of green and yellow tiles on the top of the shelf. Let dry.
7. Nip white and yellow tiles in half. Glue rectangles along bottom and sides of apron of shelf, alternating colors.
8. Glue plaster pieces on apron of shelf, using photo as a guide for placement.
9. Break and nip green tiles and glue the pieces around the plaster shapes. Let dry.

Grout:
10. Mix grout according to package instructions. Spread over tiles, bringing

the grout up to **but not over** the plaster pieces. Wipe away excess. If any grout is left on the plaster pieces, use a damp cotton swab to remove it.

11. Wipe away the haze with a soft cloth.

Finish:

12. Touch up the paint on the plaster pieces, if necessary. Apply more transparent gold paint. Let dry. Apply another coat of gloss sealer.

13. Paint shelf brackets and edges of shelf with green acrylic craft paint. Let dry.

14. Paint edges of shelf and edges of brackets with yellow acrylic craft paint. Let dry.

15. Sand the yellow-painted areas lightly to remove some of the paint and create a distressed look.

16. *To Hang:* See instructions for "Forest Dreams" Backsplash. ∾

Beauty at Your Feet

This "stepping stone" is beautiful as an outdoor or indoor accent piece. For indoor use, the stone could be cast from plaster, and white craft glue could be used to attach the tiles. It would look great in an indoor garden area.

Method: Mixed Media
Mosaic Area: 120 square inches

SUPPLIES

Cement stepping stone (or 11"
    stepping stone mold and cement)
1 hunter green tile, 4" x 4"
4 cobalt blue tiles, 2-3/4" x 2-3/4"
4 cobalt blue decorated tiles, 1-1/2" x 1"
Square tiles, 3/8", in various matching
    shades
Chinese floral pattern china plate
Mastic glue
Glue trowel
Stencils with small motifs and nature
    themes:
    Flowers
    Insects
    Turtle
    Fern fronds
    Leaves
    Frog
Permanent enamel paints (the kind that
    are baked in the oven for durability)
Sanded grout - white
Small stencil brushes
Liner brush
Mosaic sealer
Basic tools & supplies

INSTRUCTIONS

Preparation:
1. If you are molding your own stepping stone, mix cement with water according to package instructions and mold stepping stone. Let dry.
2. Stencil designs on the hunter green tile and square cobalt blue tiles. Paint details with a liner brush.
3. Bake tiles in the oven according to the instructions on the paint packaging. Let cool.
4. Break china plate into irregular pieces.

Attach Tesserae:
5. Spread mastic on stepping stone.
6. Place large, center stenciled tile and the four smaller stenciled tiles, using photo as a guide for placement.
7. Place small square tiles around large center tile and around edges of stepping stone.
8. Place the medium sized decorative tiles in the four quadrants.
9. Fill in areas between tiles with broken china. Let dry.

Grout:
10. Mix grout. Spread over tiles. Remove excess. Let dry.
11. Polish haze with a soft cloth.
12. Apply sealer. Let dry. ෴

Artful Address Sign

Method: Direct

SUPPLIES

Wooden house number sign with enough spaces to accommodate your house number (On this one, the spaces for the tile numbers are 4" x 4"; the sign is 18" long and 6" tall)

Square tiles, 3/8" (about 100 for each number on your sign):
Blue
Green
White
Beige

2 triangular tiles - blue

Sanded grout - tan

Gloss acrylic craft paint:
White
Deep blue

Gold metallic rub-on wax

White craft glue

Silicone adhesive

Graph paper & pencil

Transfer paper & stylus

Black permanent marker

Clear acrylic sealer

Grout sealer

Sandpaper, 220 grit

Tack cloth

Basic tools & supplies

INSTRUCTIONS

Preparation:
1. Sand sign smooth. Wipe away dust.
2. Apply coat of clear sealer to the areas where the tiles will be placed. Let dry.
3. On graph paper, draw your house numbers. Transfer them to sign. Go over the lines with a black marker.

Attach Tesserae:
4. Glue green tiles in the corners of each number square.
5. Glue blue and green tiles on number shapes, spacing tiles on curves as shown in photo.
6. Glue white tiles around numbers, nipping tiles as needed to fit the spaces. Let dry.

Grout:
7. Mix grout. Spread over tiles. Wipe away excess. Let dry.
8. Polish away haze with a soft cloth.

Finish:
9. Sand sign lightly to remove any grout from areas to be painted, if needed. Wipe away dust.
10. Paint front and back of sign with gloss white paint. Let dry.
11. Paint edges of sign with deep blue gloss paint. Let dry.
12. Rub metallic gold wax over blue paint.
13. Apply several coats of grout sealer to grout to protect it from weather.
14. Glue one blue triangular tile at each end of sign with silicone adhesive, using photo as a guide for placement. ∞

Teapot Collection Shelf

Method: Mixed Media

SUPPLIES

Wooden shelf
Square tiles, 7/8" (55-60 tiles of
    each color):
    Light blue
    Dark blue
China plate, blue and white pattern
China plate, pink floral pattern
Plaster or candy molds:
    Large teapot
    Small teapot
    Cup & saucer
Acrylic craft paints:
    Light blue
    Dark blue
Metallic gold rub-on wax
Clear gloss sealer
Non-sanded grout - white
Cotton swabs
Gold metallic rub-on wax
Sponge brush
Small artist's paint brush
Basic tools & supplies

continued on page 72

Teapot Collection Shelf

Pictured on page 70-71

continued from page 70

INSTRUCTIONS

Preparation:

1. Seal the areas of the shelf where the tiles will be attached. Let dry.
2. Mold the teapots and cups and saucers, following package instructions. Let dry. Unmold. Sand to smooth any rough edges.
3. Rug plaster pieces with metallic gold wax. Let dry.
4. Apply two to three coats of gloss sealer to the plaster pieces to protect the pieces when you grout.

Attach Tesserae:

5. Glue a checkerboard design of light blue and dark blue tiles on the top of the shelf. Let dry.
6. Glue light blue and dark blue tiles, alternating colors, on each end of shelf apron.
7. Nip some light blue and dark blue tiles in half. Glue rectangles along bottom apron of shelf, alternating colors.
8. Glue plaster pieces on apron of shelf, using photo as a guide for placement.

9. Break and nip china plates and glue the pieces around the plaster shapes. Let dry.

Grout:

10. Mix grout according to package instructions. Spread over tiles, bringing the grout up to **but not over** the plaster pieces. Wipe away excess. If any grout is left on the plaster pieces, use a damp cotton swab to remove it. Let dry.
11. Wipe away the haze with a soft cloth.

Finish:

12. Paint the shelf supports and the back edge of the shelf light blue. Let dry.
13. Paint the edge of the shelf and front edges of the supports with dark blue. Let dry.
14. Rub dark blue painted areas and edges of tiles with gold metallic wax.
15. Touch up the metallic gold wax on the plaster pieces, if necessary. Let dry. Apply another coat of gloss sealer to plaster pieces if you touched up the wax. ∞

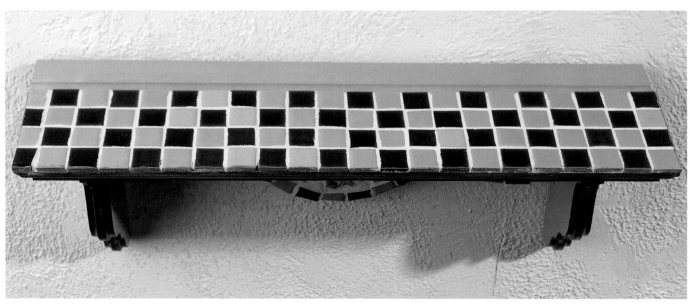

Top view of shelf

Tiled Gem Mosaic Egg

This mosaic egg is a great project for using all those tiny pieces of tile and broken china that are left over from larger projects. Wouldn't a bowl full of these eggs be fabulous? Or showcase one in a very special place.

Method: Mixed Media

SUPPLIES

Papier mache egg
Snippets of tile, broken china
12-15 square tiles, 3/8", in a variety of colors
Sanded or non-sanded grout - buttercream
Silicone adhesive
Clear acrylic sealer
Toothpicks
Basic tools & supplies

INSTRUCTIONS

1. Seal egg surface. Let dry.
2. Glue tiles and snippets of china and tile on egg with silicone adhesive, nipping pieces as needed to fit. Use enough glue to hold the pieces in place, but not so much that the glue squishes up between the pieces. (If it does, you won't be able to cover it with the grout.) Use a toothpick to remove excess glue immediately. Let dry.
3. Mix grout according to package instructions. Spread over egg, pushing the grout into all the crevices and forming a smooth, curved shape. Wipe away excess. Let dry.
4. Polish with a soft cloth to remove any haze. ❧

It's the Tops

Who would believe a round piece of plywood could be made into an object of art. This project is so easy and so much fun you won't want it to end.

Method: Direct
Mosaic Area: 325 square inches, plus about 60 black tiles
for the border around the table edge

SUPPLIES

3/4" plywood, cut to 18" in diameter
Table base
Square tiles, 7/8":
    Red
    Black
    Dark blue
    Light blue
    Yellow
    Orange
    Green
    White
Round tiles, assorted sizes, in same colors as square tiles
Brown kraft paper
Ruler
Circle template
Pencil
Colored pencils
White craft glue
Silicone adhesive
Non-sanded grout - white
Mosaic sealer
Basic tools & supplies
Optional: Spray paint for the base, tracing paper, transfer paper and stylus, black permanent marker

INSTRUCTIONS

Prepare Top and Base:
1. Seal the plywood table top. Let dry.
2. Spray paint the base, if necessary.

Plan Your Design:
3. Trace the outline of the table top on a piece of brown kraft paper. Using a ruler and circle template, draw lines and circular shapes to create a pattern. Draw circles to indicate the placement of the circular tiles. (You can use the tiles themselves as templates for this.)
4. Color in the pattern with colored pencils, using the colors of the tiles you've chosen to make a pattern for your design. Alter the design as you wish until you're pleased with the way it looks.
5. When you're pleased with the design, *either* trace it on tracing paper and transfer to the table top *or* use the pattern as a guide to create the mosaic one section at a time. If you transfer the pattern, go over the lines with a permanent marker so you can see them more easily as you work.

Attach Tesserae:
6. Working one section at a time and using white craft glue, glue circular tiles in place. Fill in around them with square tiles and pieces of square tiles. Nip or break tiles as needed to fit the design.
7. Glue black tiles around outer edge of table top with silicone adhesive. Let dry.

Grout:
8. Mix grout. Spread over tiles. Wipe away excess. Let dry.
9. Wipe away haze with a soft cloth.

Seal:
10. Seal with several coats of mosaic sealer to protect the grout from spills and the elements. ∞

See top view of table on page 76.

It's the Tops

Instructions on page 74

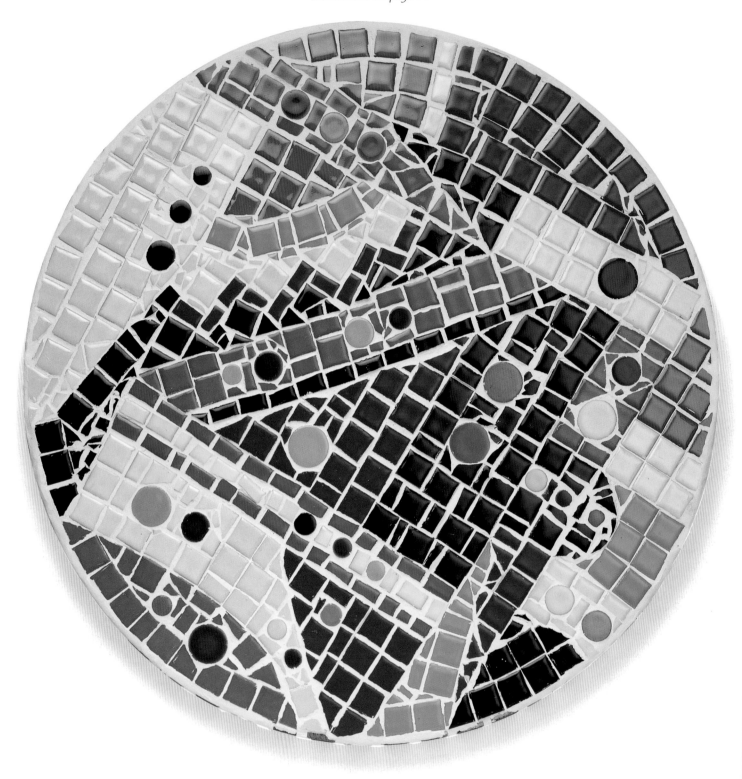

Library Mosaic Bookends

Simple wooden bookends found at a thrift shop or yard sale become a colorful accessory when decorated with tiles. Look for bookends with nice flat surfaces. Small decorated tiles can be hand painted with permanent ceramic paints or purchased at tile stores. Build the color scheme around the colors of the decorated tiles.

Method: Direct
Mosaic Area: 35 square inches (The area of each bookend is 3-1/2" x 5".)

SUPPLIES

1 pair wooden bookends
2 square decorated tiles, 2" x 2", in blues and greens
Square tiles, 3/8", in coordinating colors and white
Acrylic craft paint - deep blue
Non-sanded grout - deep blue
White craft glue
Sandpaper, 220 grit
Tack cloth
1/2" foam brush
Basic tools & supplies

INSTRUCTIONS

Preparation:
1. Lightly sand surfaces of bookends to prepare for painting. Wipe away dust.
2. Position the bookends on the edge of your work surface so you are working horizontally. Glue a decorated tile at center of each bookend.

Attach Tesserae:
3. Glue square tiles around edges to create a border, alternating colors. See photo.
4. Fill in area between border and decorated tiles with white tiles. Nip as needed to fit. Let dry.

Grout:
5. Mix grout and apply over tiles. Wipe away excess. Let dry.
6. Wipe away haze with a soft cloth.

Finish:
7. Clean grout from areas to be painted with sandpaper, if needed. Wipe away dust.
8. Paint edges with deep blue paint. Let dry. ∞

Deco Dream Table

I bought this art deco style table for $5 at a yard sale. Putting together the deco-style top is like completing a jigsaw puzzle.

Method: Direct
Mosaic Area: 330 square inches

SUPPLIES

Wooden rectangular coffee table, 24-1/2" x 13-1/2"
Square tiles, 3/4":
    Blue gray
    White
    Black
    Purple
50 square tiles, 3/8":
    Teal
    Blue
10 round tiles in coordinating colors, 1"
Non-sanded grout - purple
Gloss acrylic craft paint - black
Mosaic sealer
Sandpaper, 220 grit
Tack cloth
Black permanent marker
Basic tools & supplies

Instructions follow on page 80. Pattern is on page 82

Deco Dreams Table

INSTRUCTIONS

Preparation:

1. Sand the top of the table and prepare the rest of the table for painting. Wipe away dust with a tack cloth.
2. Trace pattern, adapting design as needed to fit your table. Transfer design to table top. Go over lines with a black marker.

Attach Tesserae:

3. Glue black and purple square tiles along long sides of table to make a border.
4. Nip black tiles in half to make rectangles and glue on both short sides to make a border.
5. Glue tiles to create chevron designs at centers of four sides and at corners. Nip tiles to fit as needed.
6. Glue round tiles in place.
7. Break or nip white, black, teal, and purple tiles. Glue to create remaining design motifs.
8. Fill in background with blue gray tiles, breaking or nipping as needed to fit. Glue in place. Let dry.

Grout:

9. Mix grout with water according to package instructions. Spread over tiles. Wipe away excess. Let dry.
10. Wipe away haze with a soft cloth.

Finish:

11. Clean away grout from wooden areas to be painted.
12. Paint legs of table and rim of table top with black paint. Let dry.
13. Apply sealer to mosaic area. Let dry. ∞

Deco Dream Table
Instructions on page 78

1 square = 1 inch

Polka Dot Pretty Lamp

Method: Direct

SUPPLIES

Black ceramic lamp base, 12-14" tall
Black paper lampshade
Round tiles, various sizes and colors, approximately 1 lb.
Braid to trim the top of the shade in a color to complement the tiles
Fabric glue
Sanded grout - black
Silicone adhesive
Basic tools & supplie

INSTRUCTIONS

1. Glue round tiles randomly to the sides of the lamp base with silicone adhesive, alternating sizes and colors of tiles. Use photo as a guide for placement. Don't use so much glue that it squishes up between the tiles. Let dry.
2. Mix grout according to package instructions. Apply to base over tiles. Wipe away excess. Let dry.
3. Polish away haze on tiles with a soft cloth.
4. Using silicone adhesive, glue a row of tiles around bottom of lamp shade, alternating sizes and colors. Let dry.
5. Using fabric glue, glue trim around top of lampshade. Let dry.
6. Place shade on base. ∾

Recycled Treasure Chair

*The chair back and sides of the apron were enhanced with tiles.
I used a decorated tile as the focal point and chose square tiles in
coordinating colors. When gluing the tiles, work one area at a time
and turn the chair so you're working on a horizontal surface.
Let dry before turning.
When choosing a chair, look for one with flat back that will
accommodate the tiles. This one was purchased at an auction.*

Method: Mixed Media
Also pictured on page 11

SUPPLIES

Wooden chair with upholstered seat
1 square decorated tile, 4" x 4"
Square tiles, 7/8" - deep blue, light blue,
    yellow, brown (about 100)
Square tiles, 3/8" - blue, green, tan, and
    gold (about 150)
Blue and white china plate
White craft glue
1 yd. blue print upholstery fabric
Gloss acrylic craft paints:
    Navy blue
    Hunter green
    Mustard
    Light blue
Non-sanded grout - buttercream
Staple gun
Sandpaper
Sponge brush
Sandpaper, 220 grit
Tack cloth
Basic tools & supplies

INSTRUCTIONS

Preparation:

1. Remove seat from chair. Remove the fabric
   from the chair seat. Save the old piece of fabric to use as a pattern for the new seat cover.
2. Prepare wood surface for painting.
3. Seal areas of wood where tiles will be
   applied. Let dry.

Attach Tesserae:

4. Using photo as a guide, glue square decorated tile in place on back of chair. Glue
   rows of square tiles around edges of back
   area.
5. Break china plate into irregularly shaped
   pieces. Glue pieces around decorated tile
   as shown in photo. Let dry.
6. Glue rows of square tiles on one side of
   chair apron. Let dry.
7. Glue rows of square tiles on other side of
   chair apron. Let dry.

Grout:

8. Mix grout according to package instructions. Spread over tiles. Wipe away
   excess. Let dry.
9. Wipe away haze with a soft cloth.

Finish:

10. Sand or chip away any grout from
    wooden surfaces to be painted. Wipe
    away dust with a tack cloth.
11. Paint chair with gloss acrylic craft
    paint. Use photo as a guide for color
    placement, adapting the placement of
    the four colors to fit your chair. Let dry
    between colors. Use as many coats as
    needed to achieve solid coverage.
12. When all the paint is dry, recover the
    seat with the new fabric, tucking to
    underside with a staple gun. Reattach
    seat to chair. ∾

Tea Time Tray

Method: Direct
Mosaic Area: 175 square inches

SUPPLIES

Wooden tray, 12" x 18"
4 square decorated tiles, 4" x 4"
Square tiles, 7/8":
    White
    Yellow
White glue
Gloss acrylic craft paint - white
Metallic acrylic craft paint - gold
Non-sanded grout - white
Mosaic sealer
1" foam brush
Basic tools & supplies
Optional: Masking tape

INSTRUCTIONS

Preparation:
1. Seal wood surface that will be covered with tiles. Let dry.
2. Position tiles on surface of tray to determine arrangement. Remove tiles.

Attach Tesserae:
3. Glue tiles in place as arranged. Place large tiles first. Glue smaller tiles around large ones. Nip tiles to fit as needed.

Grout:
4. Mix grout and apply to tiles. Wipe away excess. Let dry.
5. Wipe away haze with a soft cloth.

Finish:
6. If needed, clean away grout from wooden sides of tray. Paint inner and outer sides of tray with two coats white gloss paint. To keep paint from getting onto tiles as you paint, mask off tiles. Let paint dry between coats.
7. When final coat is dry, paint upper edges of tray and inner edges of hand holds with gold metallic paint. Let dry.
8. Apply two to three coats mosaic sealer to waterproof the grout. ∞

Timely Beauty Clock

Method: Direct
Mosaic Area: 65 square inches

SUPPLIES

Wooden birdhouse clock base,
   6-1/2" x 10-1/4"
Round clock movement and gold-
   tone bezel, 2-1/4" diameter
Square Tiles, 3/8":
   Orange
   Royal blue
   Black
   Green
   Red
   Yellow
2 square tiles, 3/8", gold
Gloss acrylic craft paint - black
1" foam brush
Metallic gold rub-on wax
Non-sanded grout - red
White craft glue
Sandpaper, 220 grit
Tack cloth
Transfer paper
Tracing paper
Pencil
Black fine tip permanent marker

INSTRUCTIONS

Preparation:

1. Set in the clock bezel in the clock base and trace around it. (This way, when your mosaic is finished, you'll have left room for it.)
2. Sand the wooden base to prepare for painting. Wipe away dust with a tack cloth.
3. Seal the area where the mosaic will be. Let dry.
4. Trace pattern, enlarging as needed. Transfer to wooden base. Go over the lines with a black marker.

Attach Tesserae:

5. Spread white glue on design one section at a time and fill in with tiles, nipping and breaking as needed to fit. Use photo as a reference for color placement and continue until the design is complete. Don't place tiles inside the line you traced for the bezel. Let dry.

Grout:

6. Mix grout according to package instructions. Spread over mosaic. Wipe away excess, being careful to remove grout from wooden areas to be painted. Let dry.
7. Wipe away haze from tile with a soft cloth.

Finish:

8. Paint the wooden roof, sides, base, entrance hole, perch and around the place where the clock movement will be with black gloss paint. Let dry. Apply a second coat, if needed to achieve complete coverage. Let dry.
9. Rub gold metallic wax along the edges of the roof and base and on the end of the perch
10. Insert clock bezel and battery. ∽

Pattern for clock is on page 111.

Sparkle & Shimmer Candle Holders

A pair of candlesticks from a yard sale is transformed with broken china. Tall, thin, rounded surfaces like these look best when you use very small pieces—so this project is a great way to use up those tiny pieces left over from other projects.

Method: Curved Surface

SUPPLIES

Wooden candlesticks, 11-1/2" tall
Pieces of broken pearlized china
Gold metallic paint
Gold metallic powder
Non-sanded grout - buttercream color (or added colorant)
Silicone adhesive
Sandpaper, 220 grit
Clear acrylic sealer
Tack cloth
1/2" foam brush
Basic tools & supplies
(Optional): Gold leaf and gold leaf adhesive, rather than gold paint

INSTRUCTIONS

Preparation:
1. Sand candlesticks lightly. Wipe away dust.
2. Seal the areas where the mosaic will be located with clear sealer. Let dry.
3. Using your nippers, create the tiny pieces of china.

Attach Tesserae:
4. Glue pieces of broken china on candlesticks with silicone adhesive. Use adhesive sparingly. Let dry.

Grout:
5. Mix some gold metallic powder with the grout to give the grout a slight glow. Mix grout with water according to package instructions.
6. Spread grout over china pieces. Wipe away excess. Let dry.
7. Polish haze from china with a soft cloth.

Finish:
8. Clean off any grout on the areas to be painted, sanding as needed. Wipe away dust.
9. Paint the top and bottom areas with gold paint. Let dry. *Optional:* Apply gold leaf adhesive and gold leaf instead of painting the top and bottom areas. ༎

Hearts & Circles Trivets

You can use any type of tiles to make trivets, but choose ones of the same thickness so the surface will be fairly even—you want a hot dish to be able to sit on the trivet securely. When you aren't using the trivet, hang it on the wall for a lovely decoration.

Trivet with Light Background

Method: Direct
Mosaic Size: 36 square inches

SUPPLIES

Black metal trivet frame with fiberboard insert, 6" x 6"
Tiles in a variety of shapes—rounds, ovals, hearts, pebbles, leaf shapes, 3/8" squares—in blues, greens, white
2 leaf tiles with veins - 1 white, 1 green
Sanded grout - buttercream
White craft glue   Sandpaper, 220 grit
Tack cloth   Paper & pencil
Optional: transfer paper   Basic tools & supplies

INSTRUCTIONS

Preparation:

1. Remove fiberboard insert from frame. Sand smooth. Wipe away dust. Trace shape of insert on a piece of paper with a pencil.
2. Seal the fiberboard base. Let dry.
3. Arrange the tiles on the paper template, making a freeform design that pleases you. Use photo as a guide. Trace around the shapes to make a pattern. *Optional:* Transfer to the fiberboard base.
4. Glue the fiberboard base into the trivet frame. Let dry.

Attach Tesserae:

5. Glue the tiles in place on the fiberboard base of the trivet, using your template or transferred pattern as a guide. Let dry.

Grout:

6. Mix grout according to package instructions. Spread over tiles. Wipe away excess, being sure to remove all traces of grout from trivet frame. Let dry.
7. Wipe away haze with a soft cloth. ∽

Dark Background Trivet — instructions on page 94.

Hearts & Circles Trivets

Pictured on page 92-93

Trivet with Dark Background

Method: Direct
Mosaic Size: 36 square inches

SUPPLIES

Black metal trivet frame with fiber-
board insert, 6" x 6"
Tiles in a various shapes—pebbles,
rounds, ovals, hearts, 3/8" squares—
in a variety of colors
5 flatbacked marbles
Sanded grout- deep blue
White craft glue
Sandpaper, 220 grit
Tack cloth
Basic tools & supplies
Optional: transfer paper

INSTRUCTIONS

Preparation:

1. Remove fiberboard insert from
frame. Sand smooth. Wipe away
dust. Trace shape of insert on a piece
of paper with a pencil.
2. Seal the fiberboard base. Let dry.
3. Arrange the tiles and flatbacked marbles on the paper template, using
photo as a guide for placing the marbles and making a design that pleases you. It's important to distribute the
marbles evenly so a hot pot or bak-
ing dish sitting on the trivet will be
secure. Trace around the shapes to
make a pattern. *Optional:* Transfer to
the fiberboard base.
4. Glue the fiberboard base into the
trivet frame. Let dry.

Attach Tesserae:

5. Glue the flatbacked marbles and tiles in place on the fiberboard base of the trivet, using
your template or transferred pattern as a guide. Let dry.

Grout:

6. Mix grout according to package instructions. Spread over tiles and marbles. Wipe away
excess, being sure to remove all traces of grout from trivet frame. Let dry.
7. Wipe away haze with a soft cloth. ∞

Enlarge pattern @127% on copy machine for actual size.

Rooster Art

Instructions on page 96

Rooster Art

Method: Direct
Mosaic Area: 130 square inches

SUPPLIES

Octagonal shaped wooden plate,
　11-1/2" across
Square tiles, 7/8":
　Green
　Orange
　Yellow
　Red
　Black
　Light blue
　Royal blue
　Pink
　White
Flatbacked marbles in complemen-
　tary colors
A few pieces of broken mirror
Sanded grout - white and black
Acrylic craft paint - red
Clear acrylic sealer
Transfer paper & stylus
Tracing paper
Pencil
Sandpaper, 220 grit
Fine tip black permanent marker
Cotton swabs
Basic tools & supplies

INSTRUCTIONS

Preparation:
1.　Sand wood. Wipe away dust.
2.　Seal wood surface with clear acrylic sealer. Let dry.
3.　Trace the pattern from this book. Enlarge or reduce the pattern on a copy machine to fit the center of your plate.
4.　Transfer the rooster design to the plate. Go over the pattern lines with a black permanent marker so you will be able to see them through the glue when placing the tiles.
5.　Nip black tiles into rectangular pieces in two different sizes—smaller ones for the inner border and larger ones for the outer border. Break other colors of tiles into irregularly shaped pieces. Nip some little pieces to create the rooster.

Attach Tesserae:
6.　Glue the tiles to create the rooster in place.
7.　Glue the smaller black tile pieces for the inner border in place.
8.　Fill in the area between the rooster and the inner border with flatbacked marbles, white tiles, and mirror pieces. Nip pieces as needed to fit.
9.　Glue the larger black tile pieces around the outer edge to form the outer border.
10.　Using photo as a guide for color placement, divide the rim into eight sections. Fill sections with pieces of orange, red, green, and yellow tiles, alternating colors as shown in photo. Let dry.

Grout:
11.　Mix black grout according to package instructions. Spread over colored tiles and black tiles in rim and borders, being careful not to get black grout in center area. Wipe away excess. Remove any grout from center area with damp cotton swabs. Let dry.
12.　Mix white grout according to package instructions. Spread over tiles in round center area. Wipe away excess. Thoroughly remove any white grout from black grout. Let dry.
13.　Wipe away haze with a soft cloth.
14.　Paint edges and back of plate with red paint. Let dry. ∽

Pattern for plate is on page 95.

Place of Honor Bowl

This is a grand way to turn an old wooden salad bowl into a piece of art.
Have fun combining scraps and snippets of china and pieces of broken tiles
with various irregularly shaped tiles to create lovely colors and shapes.

Method: Mixed Media
Mosaic Size: To determine, measure the circumference of
your bowl in inches. Multiply by the height of the
bowl in inches.

SUPPLIES

Wooden bowl
Variety of unusually shaped tiles,
    various colors
Pieces of broken tiles
Pieces of broken china
Acrylic craft paints:
    Gloss white
    Metallic gold
Silicone adhesive
Clear gloss spray sealer
Plastic wrap
Disposable plate or palette
Sanded grout - gray blue
Sandpaper, 220 grit
Tack cloth
Masking tape
Basic tools & supplies

INSTRUCTIONS

Preparation:
1. Sand bowl to smooth surface. Wipe away dust with a tack cloth.
2. Paint the bowl, inside and out, with gloss white paint. Let dry.

Attach Tesserae:
3. Glue china pieces, tile pieces, and tiles randomly to sides and bottom of bowl with silicone adhesive. Let dry.

Grout:
4. Mix grout according to package instructions. Spread over tiles and china pieces. Wipe away excess. Let dry.
5. Wipe away haze with a soft cloth.

Finish:
6. Remove any grout from the top edge or inside of the bowl. Sand if needed. Paint the inside and the top edge of the bowl with another coat of gloss white paint. Let dry.
7. Pour a little gold metallic paint on a disposable plate or palette. Cut a piece of plastic wrap about 6" x 6". Wearing a disposable latex glove, crumple the plastic, dip in paint, blot on a paper towel, and press on the inside of the bowl to create a mottled look. Continue dipping, blotting, and pressing until the inside of the bowl is mottled. Let dry completely.
8. Mask off the mosaic area with tape. Spray the inside of the bowl with one to two coats gloss sealer. Let dry. Remove tape. ⌒

Terra Cotta Treasure

This terra cotta saucer becomes a great serving piece with a Mediterranean flair. This project is a perfect way to use some broken decorated tiles and a few pieces of broken terra cotta. It's fast and easy and makes a great gift.

Method: Mixed Media

SUPPLIES

Terra cotta saucer, 8" (or size of your choice)
Broken decorated terra cotta tile with blue painted design
Broken pieces of terra cotta
Square tiles, 7/8", deep blue (about 60)
Sanded grout - tan
Silicone adhesive
Sandpaper
Basic tools & supplies

INSTRUCTIONS

Preparation:

1. Scrub terra cotta dish to remove any dirt or mold. Let dry. Sand any rough spots with sandpaper. Rinse. Let dry.

Attach Tesserae:

2. Glue two rows of blue tiles around sides of dish, using photo as a guide for spacing and placement.
3. Glue broken tile pieces and terra cotta pieces randomly on bottom of dish. Let dry.

Grout:

4. Mix grout according to package instructions. Spread over tiles and terra cotta pieces. Wipe away excess. Let dry.
5. Polish tiles with a soft cloth to remove haze. ∾

Pastoral Scene Card Box

*A broken antique plate—purchased chipped in a thrift store—is reassembled
on the lid of this card box. A decorative bead pull is used as a handle.*

Method: Mixed Media
Mosaic Area: 30 square inches

SUPPLIES

Wooden card box, 6-1/4" x 4-3/4", 2" tall
China plate with pastoral scene
8-10 pieces pink opalescent stained glass
Non-sanded grout - white
Acrylic craft paint:
    Dusty green
    Antique gold
White craft glue
Silicone adhesive
1-1/2 yds. gold self-adhesive paper lace
    trim
1-1/2 yds. pink ribbon, 1/4" wide
Decorative bead, 1/2" (for handle)
4 wooden beads, 5mm (for feet)
Sandpaper, 220 grit
Tack cloth
Basic tools & supplies

INSTRUCTIONS

Preparation:
1. Sand the box. Wipe away dust.
2. Paint the inside of the box dusty green. Let dry.
3. Paint the outside of the box and the four wooden beads antique gold. Let dry.
4. Seal the top where the mosaic will be applied with clear sealer. Let dry.
5. Nip away the rim of the china plate, reserving the pieces, leaving the center design in one piece. Break the china plate, being sure not to strike it so hard with the mallet that it shatters into little pieces—you want to be able to reassemble the scene.

Attach Tesserae:
6. Glue the china pieces on the top of the box with white craft glue, reassembling the scene. Add a few pieces of stained glass on the outer edges along with some pieces from the rim of the plate. See photo. Let dry.

Grout:
7. Mix grout with water according to package instructions. Spread over china and glass pieces. Wipe away excess. Let dry.
8. Polish haze from china pieces with a soft cloth.

Finish:
9. Touch up the antique gold paint as needed. Let dry.
10. Apply two rows of gold paper lace trim, using photo as a guide for placement.
11. Glue ribbon over trim with white craft glue. Let dry.
12. Attach bead to lid with silicone adhesive. Glue four gold-painted beads to bottom with silicone adhesive. ✑

Clear Delight Bottles & Mirror

These boudoir bottles and mirror are the ultimate in feminine glitz. Stained glass pieces, used in both grouted and ungrouted effects, create a dazzling collection for the boudoir. You can buy a mirror tray or have a glass shop cut a piece of 1/4" thick mirror glass to size and polish the edges. Use felt protectors on the bottom.

Method: Ungrouted

Ungrouted Glass Bottles & Vase

SUPPLIES

Clear or tinted glass vase
Clear or tinted glass bottles with stoppers or corks
Polished glass pieces
Silicone adhesive
Acrylic craft paint - metallic gold (for painting corks)
Organza ribbons in various colors, 1/2 yd. of each

INSTRUCTIONS

1. Be sure glass bottles are clean and dry.
2. Glue glass pieces on sides and around tops of bottles and vase with silicone adhesive. Let dry.
3. Add finishing touches.
   • Paint corks with gold paint.
   • Glue two marbles together to make a bottle stopper for a bottle with a narrow opening.
   • Glue marbles to corks and stoppers.
   • Tie bows with ribbon around necks of bottles. ∞

Mirror Tray

Method: Mixed Media
Mosaic Area: 50 square inches

SUPPLIES

Rectangular mirror, 16" x 9"
Broken pieces of stained glass:
    Blue, Purple, Gold, Green
Broken pieces of clear textured glass
Flatbacked marbles, clear and opalescent, in coordinating colors
White craft glue
Acrylic craft paint - gold
Small artist's paint brush
Sanded grout - vanilla
Small piece of fabric with tiny floral motifs
Fabric stiffener
Scissors
Silicone adhesive
Basic tools & supplies

INSTRUCTIONS

1. Clean mirror. Let dry.
2. Glue stained glass pieces at corners of mirror, using photo as a guide for placement. Intersperse the flatbacked marbles with the glass pieces. Let dry.
3. Mix grout. Spread over the mosaic area. Wipe away excess, creating a smooth, curved edge to the grout along the edge of the glass pieces. Let dry.
4. Wipe haze from glass pieces with a soft cloth.
5. Paint curved edges of grout with gold paint. Let dry.
6. Stiffen fabric with fabric stiffener. Let dry.
7. Cut out tiny floral motifs (these are pansies) from fabric. Attach here and there to mosaic with silicone adhesive. ∞

Pitcher Pretty

A broken plate, a few tiles, and flatbacked marbles decorate this metal pitcher. Use it as a pitcher or a vase. The pieces are attached with silicone glue, which works well on metal. Since the pitcher is painted with spray paint, the paint is applied before the mosaic.

Method: Mixed Media

SUPPLIES

Metal pitcher, 7"
Silver spray paint
25 square tiles, 7/8", light blue
China plate, blue and white pattern
30-35 flatbacked marbles - blues and purples
Sanded grout - buttercream
Silicone adhesive   Toothpicks
Sandpaper, 220 grit   Tack cloth
Basic tools & supplies

INSTRUCTIONS

Preparation:
1. Clean the pitcher. Sand any rough or rusted places. Wipe away dust.
2. Spray pitcher inside and out with two coats silver paint. Let dry between coats.
3. Nip the tiles in half.
4. Break china plate. Nip into smaller pieces if needed.

Attach Tesserae:
5. Glue tiles around the top of the pitcher and in rows around the center and bottom of the pitcher, alternating the tiles with flatbacked marbles. Use silicone adhesive, being careful not to apply so much adhesive that it squishes up higher than the tiles. Remove excess while wet with a toothpick.
6. Glue the china pieces on the sides of the pitcher, filling in the areas between the rows of tiles. Let dry.

Grout:
7. Mix grout. Spread over tiles and china. Wipe away excess. Let dry.
8. Wipe haze away with a soft cloth.

Finish:
9. Touch up silver paint, if needed. Mask off the mosaic before spraying. ∽

God of the North Sea
Treasure Box

Wooden dimensional motifs of the mythological god of the sea, a scallop shell, and medallions decorate a wooden box. The space around the wooden motifs is filled in by tiles, pieces of mirror, and flatbacked marbles.

Method: Mixed Media

SUPPLIES

Wooden box, 11" x 8", 7" tall

Wooden dimensional accent pieces:
  Sea god's head, 5" x 6"
  2 scallop shells, 3" x 3"
  2 medallions, 4" x 4"

Aqua stone finish spray paint

30 flatbacked marbles - orange bronze

8 square terra cotta tiles, 4" x 4", light aqua

Pieces of broken mirror

White craft glue

Sanded grout - blue

Acrylic craft paint - metallic copper

1/2" foam brush

Gold metallic rub-on wax

Cotton swabs

Sandpaper, 220 grit

Tack cloth

Basic tools & supplies

INSTRUCTIONS

Preparation:

1. Sand wooden box and wooden dimensional motifs lightly.
2. Spray motifs with several coats aqua stone finish paint. Let dry.
3. Nip or break the aqua tiles into irregularly shaped pieces.

Attach Tesserae:

4. Glue head wood piece on lid of box. Glue shell wooden pieces on front and back of box. Glue a medallion on each end of box.
5. Glue nipped tiles, broken mirror pieces, and flatbacked marbles on top and sides of box around motifs.
   - Work one side at a time, turning the box so you are always working on a horizontal surface.
   - Let the side you're working on dry before turning the box and moving on to the next side.
   - Don't glue tiles, glass, or marbles where they would prevent the hinges from opening.
   Let dry.

Grout:

6. Mix grout according to package instructions. Apply grout to tiled areas, being careful not to get the grout on the wooden motifs. If grout does get on the motifs, wipe it away gently with a damp cotton swab. Let dry.
7. Polish tile with a soft cloth to remove haze.

Finish:

8. Remove any grout from wooden edges with sandpaper. Wipe away dust.
9. Paint edges with metallic copper craft paint, using a foam brush. Use as many coats as needed to achieve complete coverage. Let dry.
10. Rub wooden dimensional pieces with gold metallic wax. ∾

Pretty Pots

Here are a variety of ways to use mosaics to decorate containers for your potted plants. As you can see, it's possible to use a pot of any size—even an old one—and give it a new look.

Pansy Flower Pot Holder & Pot

Method: Direct

SUPPLIES

Wooden flower pot holder with rope handles
3" high terra cotta flower pot, 4" diameter
Paper gift wrap with pansy motifs
150 square tiles, 3/8", in colors that coordinate with pansy colors
8 square tiles, 2", light gray
White craft glue
Acrylic craft paint:
    Lavender
    Ivory
Non-sanded grout - buttercream
Gloss decoupage medium
Sponge brush
Medium brush
Small scissors
Sandpaper, 220 grit
Tack cloth
Basic tools & supplies

INSTRUCTIONS

Preparation:
1. *If you're using an old pot,* scrub pot inside and out to remove dirt and mold. Let dry thoroughly. *If you're using a new pot,* sand surface to remove any rough spots and rinse. Let dry thoroughly.
2. Seal pot inside and out with decoupage finish. Let dry.
3. Remove rope handles. Prepare surface of wooden flower pot holder for painting. Seal areas of wood that will be covered with tile. Let dry.

Attach Tesserae:
4. Using photo as a guide for placement, glue gray tiles on sides and ends of flower pot holder. Glue rows of small tiles around and between gray tiles, using photo as a guide for placement.
   • Work one side at a time, turning flower pot holder so you are always working on a horizontal surface.
   • Let the side you're working on dry before turning and moving on to the next side. Let dry.

Grout:
5. Mix grout according to package instructions. Apply grout to tiled areas, being careful not to get the grout on the wooden areas you're planning to paint. Let dry.
6. Polish tile with a soft cloth to remove haze.

Finish:
7. Remove any grout from wood with sandpaper. Wipe away dust.
8. Paint top and legs of flower pot holder and inside rim and top edge of pot with lavender paint. Let dry. Apply a second coat. Let dry.
9. Reinstall rope handles. Secure with white craft glue.
10. Paint outside of flower pot with ivory paint. Let dry. Apply a second coat. Let dry.
11. Using small scissors, cut out pansy motifs from gift wrap. Apply decoupage medium to backs of cutouts, one at a time, and position cutouts at centers of gray tiles, at four corners of top of flower pot holder, and around rim of pot. Let dry.
12. Apply two to three additional coats of decoupage medium to gray tiles, to painted areas of flower pot holder, and to pot to seal and submerge the cutouts. Let dry between coats. Let final coat dry completely.
13. Place pot in holder. ∞

Flower Petals Pot and Buttons & Tiles Pot — instructions on page 110.

Pretty Pots

Pictured on page 109

Flower Petals Pot

Method: Curved Surface

SUPPLIES

Terra cotta flower pot, 3-1/2" diameter
Pieces of broken mirror
60 oval tiles in a variety of colors
Silicone adhesive
Sanded grout - cream
(Optional): scrub brush, sandpaper
Basic tools & supplies

INSTRUCTIONS

1. *If you're using an old pot,* scrub pot inside and out to remove dirt and mold. Let dry thoroughly. *If you're using a new pot,* sand surface to remove any rough spots and rinse. Let dry thoroughly.
2. Glue oval tiles and pieces of mirror to sides of pot with silicone adhesive, arranging the oval tile to look like flower petals. Use photo as a guide for placement. Let dry.
3. Mix grout according to package instructions and spread over tiles and mirror pieces. Wipe away excess, smoothing grout to create a rounded shape at the top of the pot. Let dry.
4. Wipe away haze with a soft cloth. ∞

Buttons & Tiles Pot

Method: Curved Surface

SUPPLIES

Terra cotta flower pot, 2-1/2" diameter
30-35 square tiles, 3/8", orange, yellow, gold, and red
40-50 round buttons, different sizes, in coordinating colors
Silicone adhesive
Cotton swabs
Sanded grout - yellow
Basic tools & supplies

INSTRUCTIONS

1. *If you're using an old pot,* scrub pot inside and out to remove dirt and mold. Let dry thoroughly. *If you're using a new pot,* sand surface to remove any rough spots and rinse. Let dry thoroughly.
2. Glue square tiles and buttons to rim of pot with silicone adhesive, alternating tiles and buttons of various colors. Glue tiles and buttons randomly on sides of pot, using photo as a guide for placement. Let dry.
3. Mix grout according to package instructions and spread over tiles and mirror pieces. Wipe away excess, smoothing grout to create a rounded shape at the top of the pot. Use damp cotton swabs to remove grout from crevices and details of buttons. Let dry.
4. Wipe away haze with a soft cloth. ∞

Metric Conversion Chart

INCHES TO MILLIMETERS AND CENTIMETERS

Inches	MM	CM
1/8	3	.3
1/4	6	.6
3/8	10	1.0
1/2	13	1.3
5/8	16	1.6
3/4	19	1.9
7/8	22	2.2
1	25	2.5
1-1/4	32	3.2
1-1/2	38	3.8
1-3/4	44	4.4
2	51	5.1
3	76	7.6
4	102	10.2
5	127	12.7
6	152	15.2
7	178	17.8
8	203	20.3
9	229	22.9
10	254	25.4
11	279	27.9
12	305	30.5

YARDS TO METERS

Yards	Meters
1/8	.11
1/4	.23
3/8	.34
1/2	.46
5/8	.57
3/4	.69
7/8	.80
1	.91
2	1.83
3	2.74
4	3.66
5	4.57
6	5.49
7	6.40
8	7.32
9	8.23
10	9.14

Pattern for Timely Beauty Clock
Instructions on page 88

Enlarge pattern on copy machine @140% for actual size.

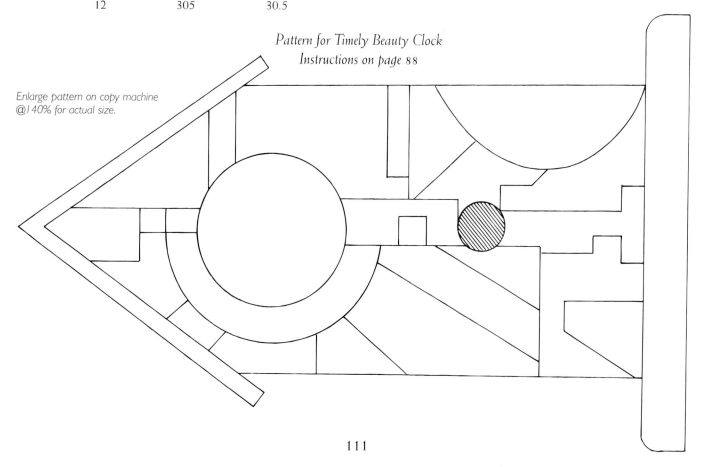

Index